WATCHING WILDLIFE

WATCHING WILDLIFE

Tips, Gear and Great Places for Enjoying America's Wild Creatures

by
MARK DAMIAN DUDA

Illustrated by
ROBERT FIELD

FALCON™

HELENA, MONTANA

Copyright © 1995 by Falcon Press Publishing Co., Inc.
Helena and Billings, Montana.

Illustrations copyright © 1995 by Robert Field.

Printed in the United States of America.

Library of Congress Cataloging-in-Publication Data
Duda, Mark Damian.
    Watching Wildlife : tips, gear, and great places for enjoying
America's wild creatures / by Mark Damian Duda ; illustrated by
Robert Field.
      p. cm.
    ISBN 1-56044-315-4
    1. Wildlife watching—North America. 2. Wildlife watching—North
America—Equipment and supplies. I. Field, Robert. II. Title.
QL60.D84   1995
599.0973—dc20   95-26073
                                                              CIP

Front cover photo: Elf Owl, Bryan Munn
Back cover photo: Moose, Michael S. Sample

Contents

ACKNOWLEDGMENTS

The wildlife management profession in North America is replete with dedicated biologists, educators, and administrators. Long hours and sometimes insurmountable conservation challenges never seem to dampen the dedication of these conservationists. As a result of their hard work and resourcefulness, North America has restored once depleted populations of white-tailed deer, wild turkeys, beavers, wood ducks, pronghorn antelope, Canada geese, and bald eagles. I can't imagine America without bald eagles or wood ducks, can you? For that reason, I dedicate this book to wildlife management professionals working for wildlife.

This book would not have been possible without the ideas, encouragement, enthusiasm, and patience of Falcon Press editor John Grassy. A dedicated wildlife conservationist, John helped develop many of the concepts presented here. Many other people offered invaluable assistance, materials, and information, including Bob Hernbrode of the Colorado Division of Wildlife. Much-appreciated assistance also came from Mark Hilliard, Bureau of Land Management; Cindy Swanson, USDA Forest Service; Nancy Marx, U.S. Fish and Wildlife Service; Deborah Richie, The Nature Conservancy/USDA Forest Service; Laury Marshall, Izaak Walton League; Dave McElveen, Florida Game and Fresh Water Fish Commission; Nancy Tankersley, Alaska Department of Fish and Game; and Wilderness Voyagers, Harrisonburg, Virginia. Kira Young, Cathy Thomas, and Rebecca Sipes of Responsive Management assisted in numerous ways and kept the project focused and organized.

I am especially grateful to Dr. Stephen Kellert of Yale for encouraging wildlife viewing as an activity and as a tool for teaching, and for teaching me the importance of managing the activity. Dr. Kellert urged me to take a closer look at wildlife viewing for my graduate work at Yale University in 1982, long before others recognized its significance.

I offer a special thank you for support and encouragement from my family: my wife Mary Anne, daughter Madeline, and son Mark Damian II. I am also indebted to Stanley and Barbara Duda, parents strong enough to allow their children to reach for dreams of their own.

1 | Wildlife Viewing in North America

A few years ago, after conducting a wildlife communications workshop in British Columbia, I elatedly received an invitation to go salmon fishing with Dr. Dave Narver, Director of the Ministry of the Environment's Fisheries Program. We left early the next morning, a clear, bright March day on the Strait of Juan de Fuca, the glasslike water stretching to the distant snow-covered mountains of Olympic National Park.

Lucky thing the view was spectacular. Although I was fishing with one of the best salmon fishermen around, the very director of the Fisheries Program, we went several hours without so much as a bite. (This has since become the source of many jokes.) As I pondered

my complete lack of angling prowess, I was startled by a large splash not fifty yards off. Another splash brought me completely out of my daydreams: a group of orcas had come upon us.

In my initial excitement I raised my arm and yelled, pointing them out to Dave—as if eighteen killer whales (each twenty-five feet long and weighing seven tons) within a stone's throw of our small boat needed pointing out. As I did so, I splashed the hot cup of coffee I was drinking all over Dave, who, until that day at least, had been an important client. What an impression I must have made.

But these were ORCAS. Their vivid black and white bodies cut the water, their large dorsal fins sliced the surface. I had always envisioned them smaller. In identification books, orcas are often pictured alongside massive blue whales or finbacks, making them appear smaller than they actually are. In the middle of the strait, viewed from a sixteen-foot runabout, they were immense.

What was most striking about the whales, however, was their sound. We were so close, so alone, and the air was so still I could hear every count of their breathing. Their massive intakes gave me a rare perspective on just how large their lungs must be. We followed them slowly for a half hour, listening and watching. Almost as quickly as they appeared, they were gone.

Wildlife viewing is one of North America's most popular and fastest-growing outdoor activities. According to National Surveys of Fishing, Hunting, and Wildlife-Associated Recreation, conducted by the U.S. Fish and Wildlife Service, the number of Americans who took trips for the specific purpose of watching wildlife increased 63 percent during the past decade. Today almost 30 million Americans take wildlife viewing trips each year. About 19 percent of Canadians take trips for the specific purpose of watching wildlife, and the Canadian Wildlife Service reports the total number of participants grew from 3.6 million to 4.4 million in the last six years, an increase of 23 percent.

We can talk about wildlife viewing in such statistical terms. But facts and figures had little to do with my morning encounter with orcas in the Strait of Juan de Fuca. On a personal level, wildlife viewing is about experiences and memories that last a lifetime. There is nothing to compare with the awe and excitement that accompany a momentary encounter with wild creatures. Despite exhaustive efforts of nature photographers, filmmakers, and writers to capture its vividness, wildlife is most fully revealed one-on-one.

WILDLIFE VIEWING AND CHILDREN

When Brian Burk of Merritt Island, Florida, was eleven years old, he spent a week at the Florida Game and Fresh Water Fish Commission's Everglades Youth Camp in West Palm Beach. There he observed deer, hawks, owls, snakes, and raccoons while at camp, and enthusiastically remarked later, "You learn more when you're outside. When you experience it, you remember it. It's better to learn about wildlife for yourself!"

Brian's experience backs up the findings of most research [see sidebar, page 14]. These show that the best way to foster positive attitudes about wildlife and the natural environment is direct participation in outdoor activities such as hiking, wildlife viewing, and bird identification.

Aldo Leopold remembered his own early experiences with wildlife. Considered by some to be the father of wildlife management in America, Leopold remarked in *A Sand County Almanac*, "My earliest impressions of wildlife and its pursuit retain a vivid sharpness of form, color and atmosphere that half a century of professional wildlife experience has failed to obliterate or to improve upon."

My three-year-old daughter, Madeline, recently demonstrated to me just how much wildlife information young children can assimilate. Madeline accompanied me during much of my fieldwork for my last book, the *Virginia Wildlife Viewing Guide*. In our travels, I often quizzed her on wildlife identification. Several months later, during Thanksgiving week, we returned to one of my favorite wildlife viewing locales, Chincoteague National Wildlife Refuge on Virginia's Eastern Shore, for a long weekend of hiking, biking, and wildlife watching. Chincoteague is a wildlife watcher's paradise. In autumn, hundreds of snow geese can be seen at one impoundment, aptly named Snow Goose Pool. During early fall, Chincoteague is one of the best places in the United States to view peregrine falcons.

Madeline and I attended a decoy festival held in the town of Chincoteague, as it is each year. World-class woodcarvers from up and down the East Coast show and sell their magnificent decoys and sculptures. My daughter walked up to one booth where a gentleman sat sculpting a decoy, making sure of the accuracy of his work.

"You know what this is?" he asked Madeline, simply looking for something to say to the child standing in front of his booth.

"Yes," she replied. "It's a Canada goose."

The eyebrows of the woodcarver rose slightly. He pointed to another decoy. "What's this one?"

"A redhead," quickly came the reply.

His curiosity was piqued. "What's this one?"

"A wood duck," Madeline said, "a boy wood duck." Then she turned and said to me, "This man doesn't know about ducks, Daddy."

THE NATIONAL WATCHABLE WILDLIFE PROGRAM

Wildlife managers across North America have noticed increasing numbers of wildlife enthusiasts. These managers have enhanced wildlife viewing opportunities in parks, refuges, forests, and wildlife management areas by constructing blinds and towers, building boardwalks through wetlands, and establishing wildlife viewing trails. They have also spread the word by producing wildlife viewing guides. These efforts have culminated in the establishment of the National

Watchable Wildlife Program, a historic partnership of state and federal conservation agencies and private conservation groups.

The National Watchable Wildlife Program encourages wildlife viewing, teaches people about wildlife, and increases public support for wildlife habitat acquisition and protection. *Sports Illustrated* magazine called the initiative "one of the most significant nationwide wildlife programs since the Endangered Species Act was signed." One goal of the program is a nationwide network of wildlife viewing sites, which will include natural areas known to offer excellent wildlife viewing and, in some cases, educational opportunities.

More than twenty states now participate in the national initiative. As you travel along the roads in these areas, look for highway signs featuring a pair of brown and white binoculars. These signs direct you to prime wildlife viewing areas that are part of the National Watchable Wildlife Program. Each viewing site you visit is just one of many in that state. Chances are, that state has published a wildlife viewing guide, with directions on how to get to each site and viewing information for anywhere from fifty to one hundred fifty other viewing areas. If you want to know if your state participates in the program, call your regional fish and wildlife agency. Or visit a local bookstore, and say you're interested in obtaining one of the state-by-state wildlife viewing guides published by Falcon Press.

THE IMPACT OF WILDLIFE VIEWING

As more and more people discover the benefits of wildlife viewing, wildlife managers across the nation have become concerned about the impact increased numbers of wildlife watchers have on the animals they wish to view.

People sometimes trample habitats and harass animals as they attempt to get a closer look or make animals "do" something. Even a few wildlife photographers get too close to bird nests or pursue animals for better shots, sometimes relentlessly; one photographer was seen throwing stones at perched birds so they could be photographed flying.

Viewers with good intentions can cause great harm. Reports have it that a few years ago in California, a group of birders made their way through a grassy marsh toward the "kick-ee-doo" call of the secretive black rail, a tiny black marsh bird with white spots on its back and a chestnut nape. Moments later the calls stopped . . . the bird had been trampled to death by the birders! At Redwoods State Park, an elk disturbed by people swam into the ocean and drowned. Bighorn sheep have lost footing and tumbled to their deaths while distracted by individuals trying to get too close. Recent research has revealed other serious problems as well, such as nest abandonment and desertion of important feeding areas, resulting from increased human pressure.

> The goal of wildlife viewing is to observe animals without interrupting their normal activities.

These situations do not have to be. Wildlife and people can coexist if wildlife viewers follow the simple guidelines set forth in this book.

Watching Wildlife was written to enhance your wildlife viewing experiences. It presents tips and techniques for observing wildlife, choosing equipment, and finding species in the wild. You'll learn about the important links between a species and its habitat and how the daily and seasonal movements of wildlife relate to viewing success. But the most important parts of the book are the sections on appropriate wildlife viewing behavior. Most wildlife viewing takes place in wild areas, where there is no audience to approve (or disapprove) of conduct. Perhaps Aldo Leopold said it best when he wrote, "Whatever his acts, they are dictated by his own conscience, rather than by a mob of onlookers. . . . Voluntary adherence to an ethical code elevates self-respect of the sportsman, but it should not be forgotten that voluntary disregard of the code degenerates and depraves him."

This book talks about this code that protects our wild creatures. And it also tells you how and where to find them. So pack up your binoculars, spotting scopes, identification guides, cameras, and this guide; gas up your car or boat; lace up your hiking boots. Then head out to enjoy one of North America's fastest growing outdoor activities—*watching wildlife*.

TAKE A CHILD WILDLIFE WATCHING

Most environmental educators and psychologists agree that adult attitudes toward the natural world are greatly influenced by childhood events. And nothing seems to foster positive attitudes toward wildlife better than direct participation in wildlife-related activities, as the following examples show:

In a study on youth and their attitudes toward wildlife, researchers from the U.S. Fish and Wildlife Service found that children who actively watched birds, fished, or hunted knew more about wildlife and the natural world than children who did not participate in these activities.

Dr. Stephen Kellert of Yale University reported that children who only learned about wildlife in classrooms or zoos had the least real knowledge about animals and had a far less ecological perspective than other children. Kellert concluded that learning about animals in school needs to be supplemented by direct encounters with animals and natural habitats, whenever possible, to impart a deeper understanding of wildlife to children.

Studying a group of Florida eighth graders, Dr. David LaHart found an important link between positive attitudes toward wildlife and wildlife-oriented activities such as camping, fishing, birding, and hunting. Of all the variables he examined, LaHart ➤

found that children who participated in hiking, birding, and wildlife photography exhibited the most actual wildlife knowledge. He also discovered that class field trips produced far greater wildlife knowledge than did filmstrips, class lectures, reading, or watching television shows about wildlife.

"Reverence and respect are hard to teach," notes Cheryl Riley of the National Wildlife Federation. "They must follow from seeing, doing, and understanding, by becoming involved."

The future of North America's wildlife depends on our children's commitment to wildlife conservation. So take a child wildlife watching. Collect bugs and butterflies with your nephew. Explore the deep woods with your daughter. Introduce children to the mysteries and beauties of the natural environment. It's fun; it's also a learning experience. You will be helping a child develop positive feelings toward wildlife that will last a lifetime.

If a child is to keep alive his inborn sense of wonder . . . He needs the companionship of at least one adult who can share it, rediscovering with him the joy, excitement, and mystery of the world we live in.

RACHEL CARSON

2 | Safe
and Responsible
Viewing

Several years ago an article in the *National Parks and Conservation* magazine caught my attention:

> During the second weekend in September, Denali National Park recorded the largest amount of traffic in the park's history. More than 1,000 vehicles passed through the Savage Creek Check Station of this remote Alaskan park.
>
> One of the main attractions of the drive through Denali is the number of animals—grizzlies, moose, Dall sheep, and caribou—that can be seen from the comfort of a vehicle. Park rangers noted, however, that the September traffic caused wildlife to retreat to quieter sections of the park. Also, vehicles killed a kit fox and a full-curl Dall sheep ram; and a line of camera-

happy tourists and their cars prevented a grizzly from crossing the road.

What was anticipated to be an enjoyable and exciting weekend of wildlife viewing turned into something quite different—especially for the wildlife.

Unfortunately the situation at Denali that weekend was not an isolated event. Deborah Richie, Watchable Wildlife Coordinator for The Nature Conservancy/USDA Forest Service, recently wrote about problems caused by tourists, hikers, campers, and wildlife watchers at Glacier National Park in Montana. During the past decade, Richie noted, "Park rangers killed twenty-three black bears, seven grizzly bears, two mountain lions, a white-tailed deer, a mule deer, and a pine marten involved in conflicts with visitors. Twenty-one people suffered injuries from grizzly bears, and three [people] died."

Seeing humpback whales breach the warm waters of the Pacific, watching orcas slice through the glass surface of an Alaskan bay, counting hundreds of snow geese on their wintering grounds—these are the privileges of wildlife viewing. With these privileges, however, comes responsibility: the responsibility to observe wild animals without disrupting or interfering with their feeding, resting, or mating behaviors.

THE CHALLENGE OF WILDLIFE VIEWING

Your goal as a wildlife viewer is to observe animals without interrupting their normal activities. Meeting this challenge also provides the greatest satisfaction. When you watch without causing a reaction, you are seeing what's truly "wild" and not causing undue harm or stress to the animal in front of you.

In many ways, this notion of leaving animals alone conflicts with messages we receive from our culture. We have seen television hosts closely interact with and even touch wild animals. We have visited petting farms where domesticated animals eat from the outstretched hands of children. And we've safely stood and watched only a few feet away from large, dangerous animals in zoos. These activities in no way resemble appropriate interactions with wildlife in the field. Zoos and petting farms force animals into our world. Wildlife viewing, on the other hand, immerses us in the animals' world.

Wildlife biologists have documented many situations in which overzealous wildlife watchers caused serious problems for the animals they were interested in viewing. The reason for this problem is that some viewers think only of their single encounter with an animal, not in terms of cumulative impact. It's critical, however, to consider not only your encounter with an animal, but the impact of all those encounters that preceded it, and all that will follow.

Here are some reasons wildlife biologists are concerned with inappropriate human-wildlife interactions:

■ On Lake Huron, researchers found that human visits to tern colonies resulted in losses of eggs to predation by gulls.

■ Analysis of data collected from Cornell University's Laboratory of Ornithology revealed that predators often follow human trails to bird nests.

■ Disturbance by hikers and picnickers in the Santa Rosa Mountains in California caused desert bighorn sheep to abandon an important water hole.

■ Studies of brown pelicans and Heermann's gulls on the coast of

Baja California showed that disturbances by recreationists seriously disrupts seabird breeding.

■ In the Gulf of Maine, boats landing or passing too close to rocky islands have caused harbor seals to become restless; some adult seals have even abandoned their pups.

■ Human disturbance in the Gulf of Maine has frightened colonial nesting birds, resulting in nest abandonment, and leaving eggs and chicks susceptible to predation.

■ On the Madison River in Yellowstone National Park, photographers disturbed nesting trumpeter swans to such an extent that the birds left their nests.

■ Nesting shorebirds such as piping plovers and terns protect their eggs from the sun by sitting on them. When human activity forces a nesting shorebird to leave its nest for an undue length of time, the developing embryos can die from overheating. On a hot day, embryos can die in three minutes or less!

■ Human disturbance can cause birds of prey to abandon their nests, leaving young to die of starvation or exposure.

■ Human disturbance of Indiana bats and other bat species that hibernate in caves is a major cause of population declines.

■ Just touching coral causes damage to this fragile animal. Well-intentioned snorkelers and divers have unwittingly allowed hands, knees, fins, and tanks to contact coral, causing irreparable damage to reefs.

■ The eggs of the threatened piping plover are so well camouflaged that many unsuspecting wildlife viewers have stepped on and crushed them.

■ At Glacier National Park in Montana, ardent wildlife watchers have caused mountain goat kids to become separated from their mothers. This can happen several times a week. Unable to nurse as frequently as necessary, the goat kids lose the strength they need to escape danger. Other times, kids have run into oncoming traffic after being frightened by wildlife viewers.

No wildlife viewer wants to play a part in any of these incidents. Most inappropriate actions occur for two reasons. First, the thrill of the moment often pushes enthusiastic wildlife viewers to get closer and closer to animals. Second, some viewers just don't understand the long-term impacts of their actions. Perhaps the best advice comes from the California Department of Fish and Game, which suggests, "Always ask yourself, 'Will my presence or actions here harass some creature or displace it from its home? Is it okay for me to be here?' There's a fine line between viewing and victimizing wildlife." The Alaska Department of Fish and Game makes another important point. It notes, "Alarm cries and displays are an animal's request that you keep away."

Research indicates that wildlife's tolerance of people varies by species, season, reproductive and nutritional state, and by the degree to which the animals are accustomed to humans. Remember, energy that an animal uses to escape disturbances made by people is no longer available for other activities, such as escaping predators, attracting a mate, migrating, or raising young. Although the animal might easily compensate for a single, short disturbance, repeated disturbances add up to higher and higher energy costs. The animal may not be able to afford losing so much energy.

WILDLIFE WARNING SIGNS

Communication plays an important role in the lives of wild animals, just as it does in our world. To avoid placing wildlife in jeopardy, you need only watch and listen—if you do something inappropriate, the animal will usually let you know. Here are some of the signals used by wild animals to tell us when they feel threatened or disturbed:

Universal signals. Animals will:

■ Walk or run away (or fly, crawl, slither, hop, or swim away)

■ Charge or threaten viewers
■ Stop feeding
■ Raise their heads and look at the disturbance
■ Appear nervous
■ Suddenly stand up from a resting position
■ Change their direction of travel

Some signals used by mammals:

■ Looking at you with their ears pointed in your direction
■ White-tailed deer stomp their feet
■ Woodchucks and marmots whistle
■ Pronghorn antelope flare their white rump patches
■ Beavers slap their tails on the water
■ Grizzly bears may charge, and have killed people who come too close

Some signals used by birds:

- Exhibiting a "broken-wing" display
- Circling repeatedly
- Crying out overhead
- Diving at intruders
- Freezing
- Ducks pump their heads
- Young owls sway from side to side and "pop" their beaks
- Canada geese hiss and charge

JOHN JAMES AUDUBON, ARTIST AND WILDLIFE VIEWER

For a perfect conception of their beauty and elegance, you must observe them [trumpeter swans] when they are not aware of your proximity, as they glide over the waters of some secluded island pond. The neck, which at other times is held stiffly upright, moves in graceful curves, now bent forward, now inclined backwards over the body. The head, with an extended scooping movement, dips beneath the water, then with a sudden effort it throws a flood over its back and wings, while the sparkling globules roll off like so many large pearls. The bird then shakes its wings, beats the water, and, as if giddy with delight, shoots away, gliding over and beneath the surface of the stream with surprising agility and grace. Imagine a flock of fifty [trumpeter] swans thus sporting before you. I have more than once seen them, and you will feel, as I have felt, happier and freer of care than I can describe.

JOHN JAMES AUDUBON

THE GOLDEN RULES OF WATCHING WILDLIFE

Respect wildlife.
Respect wildlife habitat.
Respect other wildlife viewers and property.
Respect the WILD in wildlife

RESPECT WILDLIFE

The welfare of wildlife must always come first. To respect the wild animals and birds you view, follow these guidelines:

View wild animals from an appropriate distance. Always be aware of the distance between you and the animal you are watching—for the animal's protection and, in many cases, for your own. An appropriate viewing distance depends upon various factors, including the particular species, the temperament of the individual animal, and even the time of day and time of year of the encounter. A cow moose with young in spring is particularly dangerous. A nesting bird is especially susceptible to human disturbance.

What is an "appropriate" distance? Many national parks and refuges maintain viewing distance guidelines for selected species; check with a ranger or the visitor center before you take to the field. In many other places, however, you will have to judge the appropriate viewing distance on your own. In this situation, the primary rule is to view from a distance the animal feels comfortable with. Closely observe the animal for any of the warning signs described earlier. Has it stopped feeding? Is it acting skittish or nervous? If the answer is yes, you are too close.

Don't depend completely on warning signs, however. Some animals, such as bison, will charge without benefit of a warning. Be sure you are far enough away to avoid any sudden charges. (See page 27 for more on viewing large animals.)

The best way to bridge the distance between you and wild animals is to use binoculars, spotting scopes, and zoom lenses.

Stay clear of nests, dens, and rookeries; they are especially vulnerable to human disturbance. Many parent birds will abandon a nest with eggs if they are repeatedly flushed; there is a higher likelihood of predation if the parent is away from the nest. Flushed birds also give visual clues to predators about a nest's location; many predators follow human scents to nests.

Predators are not the only danger; some frightened birds refuse to feed their young. Nesting herons often regurgitate food when disturbed and numerous young herons have died of starvation as a result.

Use calls or whistles selectively. Calls, whistles, and recordings interrupt an animal's normal routine. Use calls selectively, and only with common species. Never use calls during times of mating or times of stress, such as winter.

Artificial calls are not allowed in national parks.

Never touch "orphaned" or sick animals, or wildlife that appears to be tame. Young wild animals that appear to be alone usually have parents waiting nearby.

Limit your stay. Most encounters with people stress an animal, even if no outward signs are visible. Like any good visitor, limit your stay and let the animal get back to its normal routine.

Avoid surprising wildlife. Never try to sneak up on an animal. A startled animal is stressed, and potentially dangerous. Sneaking up on an animal puts you in a predatory role, so you will be treated as a predator by that animal.

Don't litter. Litter is ugly and no one wants to look at it. But there's another reason not to litter: animals may eat the garbage left on the ground, whether it is edible or not. Since most human litter is from food and food wrappings, the garbage smells like something to eat. Animals will try to do so, but often become ill and die.

Animals also can become entangled in litter. Six-pack holder rings from soft drinks or beer are particularly disastrous. One of the most pathetic sights I ever witnessed was a Canada goose with its head stuck in one of these holders, thrashing about and choking.

Trash and food scraps on beaches where piping plovers nest attract predators that prey on plover eggs and chicks. Predation is a major reason for this beautiful bird's decline.

Burying garbage and food is a form of littering. Pack out what you pack in.

Leave pets at home. Your pets will startle, chase, and even kill wildlife. Do not bring them into the wild.

Not only do pets decrease your chances of seeing wildlife, you may also be placing your pet in jeopardy, since wild animals have been known to maim and kill pets while being harassed.

Don't whack trees, pound bushes, or use other methods to rouse animals. Some birders use a method known as tree-whacking to rouse cavity-dwelling birds. Don't do it. Throwing stones or other objects to goad animals is also highly inappropriate.

Never feed wild animals [see page 31].

RESPECT WILDLIFE HABITAT

When you watch wildlife outdoors, you enter an animal's home. Keep in mind the impacts you may be having on wildlife habitat, and minimize your effect by doing the following:

Stay on the trail. Using existing trails and pathways minimizes habitat trampling. Staying on trails also decreases your chances of getting lost. Don't take shortcuts across switchbacks when hiking in hilly or mountainous country; this damages vegetation and causes soil erosion.

Staying on trails also helps you to walk more quietly, increasing your likelihood of seeing wildlife.

Use restrooms. Human waste is a serious pollutant. It's important to think of it in terms of cumulative impact: urine along trails and roadsides can create salt concentrations that attract animals and habituate them to people. This is a problem in many national parks, including Glacier. Schedule and plan restroom visits, especially when in large groups.

Do not rearrange or disturb foliage around dens or nests. Don't rearrange foliage for a better view of a nest or den. By making a den or nest more visible to people, you also make it more visible to predators.

Leave the habitat better than you found it. Carry along a trash bag and pick up litter when you see it. I'll never forget watching herpetologist David Cook scale down several large boulders to pick up someone else's garbage while on a wildlife watching trip; he didn't think anyone else was watching as he quietly placed the litter in his pack. We can all learn from his actions.

RESPECT OTHER WILDLIFE VIEWERS AND PROPERTY

Wildlife viewing is a popular activity; don't be surprised if you encounter other people in the field. A little cooperation will go a long way. Keep the following tips in mind:

Respect the rights of others while in the field. If you approach too closely and scare an animal away, you ruin everyone's wildlife viewing experience. Large groups can schedule periods of silence so that animals are not frightened.

Don't monopolize the sightlines. If viewing in a crowd, take a look at the animal being observed, then let the next person have a turn.

Respect the rights of landowners. Always get permission before entering private property. Be courteous and leave gates and other property as you found them.

Spread the word about appropriate wildlife watching behavior. Teach others, especially children, about the importance of not disturbing wildlife while viewing.

RESPECT THE **WILD** IN WILDLIFE

Keep your distance from all animals, especially large ones such as bears, moose, mountain lions, alligators, and bison. Don't be lulled into a false sense of security by other people moving closer and closer to an animal, and don't think you are somehow protected because you are in a park or refuge.

Wild animals are just that—wild. These tips on respecting wild animals will help you enjoy your wildlife watching experience:

Do not approach large animals. In general, maintain a distance of at least one hundred yards from large mammals. Moose, bison, and bears can run at speeds of thirty-five miles per hour. The Center for Wildlife Information warns, "Moose will charge—running, kicking, and stomping—when they feel threatened. It only takes a small provocation (a person's approach, a dog's bark, or the scent of a coyote) to change a passive moose into a dangerous one."

Regarding bison, the Center notes, "Buffalo may look slow but are very fast. They also have short tempers. Buffalo will stomp, and use their horns and their massive body weight to gore or otherwise injure what they consider a threat."

Don't learn the hard way. Keep your distance.

Stay clear of a mother with young. No matter what, never approach a mother with young. Never allow yourself to get between a sow bear and her cubs; mother black bears warn their cubs of danger with a "woof," then turn to what they see as a threat. A cow moose also can become one of the most dangerous animals when protecting her young. During spring, be safe and assume a female moose, deer, or bear has young hidden nearby, and move away immediately.

Never surround an animal with a group of people. Large groups of people, led by the thrill of the moment, often surround an animal they are observing. Large mammals have been known to charge right through such crowds because they feel cornered, causing major injuries to wildlife watchers. Always give animals a way to escape.

Be aware of tides. While viewing in coastal areas, always be aware of tidal conditions. "Incoming tides can cut off your return route," notes the National Park Service. Never attempt to beat the tide.

Practice safety during hunting season. Fourteen million Americans and almost two million Canadians enjoy hunting each year. If you decide to view wildlife in areas where hunting is taking place, follow the same safety rules that hunters follow, such as wearing hunter orange. Since animals are much more wary during hunting season anyway, making wildlife observation more difficult, consider finding an alternative area where hunting is not allowed, such as a national park or urban refuge.

Know how to act around black bears, grizzly bears, and mountain lions. The chances of a negative encounter with a mountain lion, grizzly bear, or black bear, are exceedingly small. In fact, the chances of even **seeing** a mountain lion are low, even for the most experienced backcountry traveler. If you do encounter a mountain lion or bear, stay safe.

The Colorado Division of Wildlife notes that there are no definite rules about what to do if you meet a black bear or mountain lion, and that every situation is different, but it offers the following advice.

If you meet a mountain lion:

■ Do not approach it, especially one that is feeding or with kittens. Most mountain lions will try to avoid a confrontation.

■ Give it a way to escape.

■ Stay calm.

■ Talk calmly yet firmly to the lion.

■ Move slowly. Stop, then back away slowly, only if you can do so safely. Running may stimulate a lion's instinct to chase and attack.

■ Face the lion and stand upright, doing all you can to appear larger. Raise your arms and open your jacket if you're wearing one.

■ If you have small children with you, protect them by picking them up so they won't panic and run.

■ If the lion behaves aggressively, throw stones, branches, or whatever you can get your hands on without crouching or turning your back. Wave your arms slowly and speak firmly.

What you want to do is convince the lion you are not prey, and that you may in fact be a danger to the lion. Fight back if a lion attacks you.

If you meet a black bear:

■ Stay calm. If the bear hasn't seen you, calmly leave the area. As you move away, talk aloud to make the bear aware of your presence.

■ Back away slowly while facing the bear. Avoid direct eye contact, since bears may perceive this as a threat.

■ Give the bear plenty of room to escape. Wild bears rarely attack people unless they feel threatened or provoked.

■ If on a trail, step off the trail on the downhill side and slowly leave the area. Don't run or make any sudden movements. Running is likely to prompt the bear to give chase and you can't outrun a bear.

■ Speak softly. This may reassure the bear that no harm is meant to it.

■ Try not to show fear.

Bears use all their senses to try to identify what you are. Their eyesight is good and their sense of smell is excellent. If a bear stands upright or moves closer, it may be trying to detect smells in the air. This is not a sign of aggression. Once the bear identifies you, it may leave the area or try to intimidate you by charging to within a few feet before it withdraws. Fight back if a black bear attacks you.

The situation changes if you meet a grizzly bear. The Interagency Grizzly Bear Committee, the U.S. Fish and Wildlife Service, and the Wyoming Game and Fish Department teamed up to offer the following advice.

If you meet a grizzly in the backcountry:

■ First, try to back out of the situation. Keep calm, avoid direct eye contact, back up slowly, and speak in a monotone. Never turn your back on the bear and never kneel. Never run, and do not climb a tree unless you have time to climb at least ten feet before the bear reaches you. Remember, bears can run very fast. If you do have time to climb a tree, you may want to drop a nonfood item, such as a camera, to distract the bear while you climb.

■ If the bear charges, stand your ground. Bears often "mock charge" or run past you. The bear may charge several times before leaving the area. Shooting a bear when it is charging is not recommended. The bear almost always lives long enough to maul the shooter severely.

■ As a last resort, play dead. Curl into a ball, covering your neck and head with your hands and arms. If you have a backpack, leave it on; it will help protect your back. If the bear swats at you, roll with it. Stay in a tucked position and do not look at the bear or your surroundings until you are sure it is gone. Playing dead will not work in an encounter with a grizzly bear in camp.

WHY NOT FEED THE ANIMALS?

The sign reads PLEASE DO NOT FEED THE ANIMALS. But why not?

Feeding wild animals is fun, especially for children, isn't it? Wild animals like potato chips, don't they? Why shouldn't I feed those "hungry" animals? It's no big deal, is it?

Yes, it is. There are many good reasons for never feeding wild animals:

Animals that are fed by humans learn to associate people with food. Wild animals that become dependent on handouts often approach cars, making them more likely to be hit by vehicles. Hundreds of animals are struck by cars each year in parks and refuges as they approach for an easy meal.

When potentially dangerous animals associate people with food, disaster can strike. Consider the following from Florida's *Saint Petersburg Times*:

> *Some residents of the Port Charlotte subdivision where a four-year-old girl was killed by an alligator on Saturday had frequently fed marshmallows to gators in the area, a state wildlife official said Monday.*
>
> *"We overheard one individual in the crowd that was there that night* [when the girl died] *talking about how that gator*

31

*looked like the one he had been feeding," said Lieutenant Jim
Farrior of the Florida Game and Fresh Water Fish Commission.*

Animals that are fed by humans lose their natural fear of people. Wild
animals unafraid of people are more likely to be involved in harmful
interactions, biting, kicking, or attacking wildlife viewers. When this
happens, the offending animal loses—it is usually destroyed. In
Yellowstone National Park, many people have been seriously injured
and some have even been killed as a result of people feeding bears.
One Yellowstone black bear was killed accidentally by a rubber bullet
fired by a ranger to scare it away from a heavily used section of the
park: the bear had been lured to the area with food by a wildlife
photographer interested in "getting a good shot."

Animals that are fed by humans can destroy the environment. At Crater
Lake National Park in Oregon, people feeding golden-mantled ground
squirrels and birds have contributed to the erosion of the rim of this
strikingly beautiful lake. Well-fed on potato chips, cheese curls, and
raisins, the park's birds and squirrels have dramatically reduced their
consumption, collection, and storage of pine seeds. Under natural
conditions, these animals collect pine seeds and thus help distribute
and plant the next generation of trees along the lake. The trees stabilize

the soil, preventing erosion. Now that more potato chips are eaten, fewer seeds are gathered, and there are fewer pine trees stabilizing the rim. The National Park Service at Crater Lake notes, "The [natural] chain has been broken."

Animals that are fed by humans cause property destruction. In Yosemite National Park in California, bears conditioned to human food cause almost $200,000 in property damage per year. Who knows?—your car, cabin, and camping or hiking equipment might be next.

Animals that are fed by humans may become unnaturally distributed in the environment. Studies conducted at Canyonlands and Arches national parks in Utah indicate that additional food at campgrounds has led to unnatural mammal distributions, disrupting the natural balance of the ecosystem.

Animals that are fed by humans are more likely to eat plastic wrappers and other litter. Eating litter can seriously harm an animal's digestive system, and in many cases leads to the animal's death.

Animals that are fed by humans can spread disease. Animals can carry diseases, such as bubonic plague or rabies, that can be transmitted to humans.

Animals that are fed by humans often are malnourished and forget how to find natural food for themselves. In some cases, wild animals that habitually eat human food lose their ability to digest natural food, and may become malnourished.

Wild animals fed by humans often become dependent on handouts. When the unnatural food source disappears, as it frequently does when park visitation diminishes in winter, such animals face starvation.

Animals that are fed by humans are more likely to become victims of poaching. Wild animals that become used to handouts are more likely to approach people, increasing their odds of becoming the victims of poachers.

It's illegal. In many states, feeding certain species is a criminal act punishable by fines and/or imprisonment. Feeding wildlife in national parks and refuges is illegal.

Feeding wildlife is a no-win situation. Please don't feed the animals!

MULE DEER AT GRAND CANYON ARE DYING TO BE FED

In Grand Canyon National Park, park rangers have been forced to kill mule deer that become hooked on junk food left by hikers and campers. The deer develop extreme addictions to junk food and lose their ability to digest natural vegetation. Left in extremely poor health, the deer must be killed. According to David Haskell, chief of resource management at Grand Canyon National Park, junk food is "the crack cocaine of the deer world."

3 | Gear up:
Essentials and
Planning

Nothing will make you a better wildlife watcher than learning all you can about wildlife behavior and habitat; this knowledge is the very best wildlife viewing "gear" you can own. You'll then be ready to accentuate the positive by acquiring the right maps, clothes, and equipment.

Whether a wildlife viewing trip lasts a day or a week, careful planning and the right gear pays off in terms of comfort, time saved, and viewing success. Since many viewing locales are remote and have no facilities, wildlife watchers should review information about an area before a visit, checking for warnings about roads, seasonal closures, dangerous wildlife, and available facilities. Make reservations

for wildlife tours or request access to restricted areas well in advance. Many people enjoy wildlife viewing, and wildlife tours and sites are in great demand.

MAPS

Always bring along good maps. Most state tourism departments offer free state maps, and you may purchase a DeLorme Atlas & Gazetteer for your state. These atlases include topographic maps that include most back roads. DeLorme maps are sold in many stores and catalogs; you may also buy one by calling (800) 227-1656 and asking for individual atlas sales. Obtain site maps from the park or refuge managers.

Ask questions about the area you plan to visit. Site managers can tell you most of what you need to know. Most travel destinations have convention and visitors bureaus that offer free information on accommodations, restaurants, campgrounds, and more. Many of these visitors bureaus have teamed up with state fish and wildlife agencies and other conservation groups to develop materials about local wildlife viewing.

THE FALCON PRESS WATCHABLE WILDLIFE® SERIES

Falcon Press of Helena, Montana, has teamed up with Defenders of Wildlife, state and federal resource agencies, and other conservation organizations to produce a series of state-specific wildlife viewing guides. Currently available for twenty-one states, these guides feature the best wildlife viewing sites in each state, with specific information on the types of wildlife most likely to be observed and the times of year various species may be seen. You'll also find directions to each site and important information on facilities. Color photos in each guide highlight popular wildlife species. Plus, a portion of the proceeds goes to wildlife conservation efforts.

To order, or for more information, contact Falcon Press Publishing Company, P.O. Box 1718, Helena, MT 59624; phone (800) 582-2665.

FIELD GUIDES

Field guides help you positively identify many of the animals you will see. Look for field guides on birds, mammals, reptiles, amphibians, fish, trees, plants, and wildflowers. The Peterson, Audubon, and Golden field guide series are the most popular and most informative guidebooks. I am often asked which series is the best. My answer is that I could not get by without any of them.

The Peterson field guide series is excellent for immediate identification—arrows and italics provide at-a-glance identification of each species' distinctive field marks. The Audubon series features color photographs and organizes species by habitat type. Golden guides have range maps on the same page as the species drawings, helping readers find what plants and animals inhabit their region.

Other reference books can be as valuable. The National Geographic Society *Field Guide to the Birds*, for instance, is an excellent guide with exquisite illustrations.

CHECKLISTS

Many parks and refuges produce checklists of animals found within their boundaries. Many state fish and wildlife agencies also produce checklists of wildlife within their state or region. Checklists contain information on what species occur, when they occur, how common they are during each season, and whether they nest or live on the site.

To get one of these invaluable checklists, call or write the location you will be visiting and ask to have one mailed to you. Or ask for a checklist at the visitor center/ranger station when you arrive, or get one from your state fish and wildlife agency. Checklists usually are available for birds, mammals, amphibians and reptiles, and fish.

LIFE LISTS

Many wildlife watchers, especially birders, keep a list of wildlife species they have seen. Often referred to as "life lists," these may be simple listings of species observed or more elaborate notated lists, including such information as season, date, time, location, habitat type, weather conditions, and behavior of the animal. Taking field notes requires careful observation and helps you learn about different species.

OTHER SOURCES OF WILDLIFE VIEWING INFORMATION

Wildlife viewing information has proliferated during the past five years. Much of this information is free. Contact your state fish and wildlife agency, or any of the large land management agencies listed below, for more information on "Watchable Wildlife."

National Parks

Yellowstone, Grand Canyon, Yosemite, Shenandoah . . . our national parks are some of the most beautiful places in North America, with 83 million acres of wildlife viewing opportunities. National parks are administered by the National Park Service of the U.S. Department of the Interior. Although some national parks are crowded in certain places, a one- or two-mile hike off the beaten path will often lead to less crowded, even remote areas. National parks tend to be heavily used at certain times of the year and virtually empty at others. Plan your trip accordingly and enjoy our national park system, the envy of the world. For more information about our national parks, contact the National Park Service, Interior Building, P.O. Box 37127, Washington, DC 20013-7127; phone (202) 208-6843.

The National Wildlife Refuge System

The U.S. Fish and Wildlife Service is the principal agency through which the federal government carries out its responsibilities to conserve, protect, and enhance the nation's fish and wildlife and manage their habitats for the continuing benefit of people. The National Wildlife Refuge System is managed by the U.S. Fish and Wildlife Service to meet this goal. As a network of more than 90 million acres of land and water in the United States, it contains almost five hundred national wildlife refuges that provide critical wildlife habitat from Alaska to the Florida Keys, and from the Caribbean to the central Pacific.

Although almost every type of habitat is represented in the NWR system, most refuges are located along four major waterfowl migration flyways, providing important feeding and resting areas during spring and fall migrations. Besides their crucial role for migratory birds, the refuges are managed for protection of endangered plants and animals, preservation of diversity, and education—they serve as places for people to better understand and enjoy wildlife. For details about these protected lands, contact the U.S. Fish and Wildlife Service, 4401 North Fairfax Drive, Webb Building, MS 130, Arlington, VA 22203; phone (703) 358-1700.

Bureau of Land Management

The Bureau of Land Management manages almost half of all federally owned lands. The BLM's National Watchable Wildlife Program was designed to increase opportunities to photograph, study, or view more than three thousand wildlife species on 270 million acres of BLM-administered land. Current goals of the Watchable Wildlife Program are to promote enhanced opportunities to view and enjoy wildlife; promote learning about wildlife and its needs; and strengthen public support for wildlife conservation and management. For more information, contact the Bureau of Land Management, 1849 C Street NW, Washington, DC 20240; phone (202) 343-5717.

National Forests

The USDA Forest Service administers our national forests and national grasslands. This agency is responsible for the management of resources on 191 million acres of land—an area about the size of Utah, Colorado, and Wyoming combined. National forests are habitat to more than ten thousand plant and three thousand wildlife and fish species.

The Forest Service's "NatureWatch" program enhances wildlife watching opportunities for people, helping them experience wildlife, fish, and plant resources. It also encourages the public to learn about and support conservation efforts. For details, contact the USDA Forest Service, P.O. Box 96090, Washington, DC 20090-6090; phone (202) 205-0957.

National Marine Sanctuaries

From the Hawaiian Islands Humpback Whale National Marine Sanctuary to the Florida Keys National Marine Sanctuary, the marine sanctuary system offers wildlife watchers numerous viewing opportunities in a marine environment. Its twelve sanctuaries are designed to promote comprehensive management of ecological, historical, recreational, and aesthetic resources.

The National Marine Sanctuaries are administered by the Sanctuaries and Reserves Division of the National Oceanic and Atmospheric Administration, U.S. Department of Commerce. The sanctuaries produce several excellent wildlife watching brochures; be sure to pick up the brochure on whale watching at the Hawaiian Islands Humpback Whale National Marine Sanctuary, (808) 541-3184, and the coral identification guide you can take underwater, produced in cooperation with The Nature Conservancy and the Florida Advisory Council on Environmental Education. Contact the National Oceanic and Atmospheric Administration, National Ocean Service, Sanctuaries and Reserves Division, 1305 East-West Highway, 12th Floor, Silver Spring, MD 20910; phone (301) 713-3074.

National Estuarine Research Reserve System

Estuaries are places where rivers meet the sea. The National Estuarine Reserve System is dedicated to fostering a system of estuary reserves that represents the wide range of coastal and estuarine habitats found in the United States. Currently the system provides 425,000 acres in seventeen states, all dedicated to protecting, managing, and providing excellent wildlife viewing opportunities. The system works with federal and state authorities to establish, manage, and maintain reserves, and to provide for their long-term stewardship. Contact: Sanctuaries and Reserves Division, Office of Ocean and Coastal Resource Management, National Oceanic and Atmospheric Administration, Washington, DC 20235; phone (202) 482-3384.

State Lands

Each state maintains a system of parks, forests, and wildlife management areas. Most state fish and wildlife agencies have developed areas for wildlife viewing and offer assistance for viewers who need more information. For example, the Colorado Division of Wildlife's Watchable Wildlife Program produces an enormous amount of information on how, when, and where to view wildlife; the Florida Game and Fresh Water Fish Commission's Nongame Wildlife Program publishes checklists of birds, mammals, reptiles, and amphibians, as well as a newsletter featuring wildlife viewing activities. Contact the fish and wildlife agency in your state or one you are planning on visiting. Generally, wildlife viewing material is available through the state government's nongame or watchable wildlife program.

SCENTS AND SUNGLASSES

When you view wildlife in warmer months, you often enter the domain of mosquitos, flies, ticks, chiggers, and other less-appealing creatures. Pack insect repellent. You'll need it.

Many animals have an excellent sense of smell, so wear unscented lotions when you can and limit the use of perfume and cologne. You may wish to mask your natural odors as well. Outdoor specialty shops sell scent blockers that inhibit human scent.

Wear sunglasses to protect your eyes from UV rays. Polarized sunglasses facilitate wildlife viewing in and around water, so can help you view fish and aquatic or marine mammals. Sunglasses also help you spot birds overhead. However, don't wear sunglasses that glint or shine when the sun hits them—they will alert animals to your presence.

Packs and Bags

For longer trips, pack along a canteen of water and snacks. Daypacks are good for carrying these items. And don't forget to pack trash bags to carry out garbage—your own and that of others you may find on the trail.

Clothing

Poor clothing choices will leave you uncomfortable; you'll end up either cold, wet, or hot. Poorly chosen clothing may also frighten away animals. The following information will help you pack wisely.

It is always better to have too much clothing with you than not enough. You can get hypothermia in fifty-degree weather if it's windy and rainy and you are not dressed properly. Dressing well means being conscious of how quickly weather can change; I've started watching wildlife on a morning when it was 60 degrees Fahrenheit and returned in 30-degree weather!

Boots

A good pair of sturdy shoes or boots is essential if you watch wildlife in more rugged country. Never hike in new boots. To break them in before you hit the trail, walk a mile or two every other night around your neighborhood.

The type of boot you should purchase depends on where you will be going and what you will be doing. Generally the more difficult the terrain, the stiffer the sole of the boot should be. The stiffer the sole, the heavier the boot. Light boots are nice because they have less break-in time and tend to cost less; heavier boots provide more support. If you don't need the support of a heavy boot, choose something lighter. Lighter boots have less environmental impact, especially off trail.

All boots should fit snugly, offer good traction, and provide ankle support. Never buy ill-fitting boots. Base your decision on the advice of a knowledgeable person, such as one of the staff at an outdoor specialty shop, in conjunction with your own gut feeling. When you slip on a pair of boots that fit the way they should, you'll know it.

Socks

Layer socks to wick away moisture, provide cushioning, and hold in warmth. Some synthetic materials have been used to make socks of medium weight that do all three of these things.

Hats

You'll need a hat and sunscreen for wildlife viewing near the shore or in more open areas. A hat with a brim that hides your eyes is a good choice, since a pair of staring eyes often signals danger to a wild animal.

The best fabrics for warm weather hats are cotton and cotton/synthetic blends, because they are cooler. For cold weather, purchase something made from a synthetic fabric that breathes and is waterproof. Do not wear a winter hat made of cotton. Cotton is not water repellent; if it gets wet, it doesn't dry easily. Wool continues to breathe and keeps your head warm, but is not as comfortable as some synthetics. Whatever type of cold-weather hat you find, be sure to wear it. Much of your body heat can escape through the top of your head.

Colors and Camouflage

When selecting clothing to wear outdoors, choose colors that match your surroundings. Earth tones and drab colors—browns, greens, dark grays—work best in most environments; white parkas are excellent in snow. The key is to consider what you look like from an animal's point of view. In the woods, a white shirt sticks out like a sore thumb. Also consider the sounds your clothing makes: hard-surfaced synthetic fabrics tend to be noisy in the cold. Quieter clothing will not disturb wildlife.

You may wish to wear camouflage clothing in an environment where there are lots of broken shadows. Camouflage garb and fabric can be found in army surplus stores and outdoor specialty shops. Consider wearing camouflage gloves and hanging camo mesh from your hat to keep animals from seeing your eyes.

But remember that camouflage isn't meant to be used every day. Bob Hernbrode of the Colorado Division of Wildlife points out that it is a specialized fabric. He says, "Washing 'camo' with most household detergents can create clothing that, to the eyes of many wild animals, almost 'glows' in low-light situations. This is because the color brighteners in detergents enhance the ultraviolet (UV) part of the light and color spectrum, which many animals see better than we do." Hernbrode suggests using old-fashioned natural soaps, or soaps that mute the UV colors. These soaps can be purchased in outdoor supply houses or through catalogs.

Dressing in Layers

Dress in layers when you head outdoors for any length of time.

The first layer—the layer closest to your skin—should "wick" moisture away from the skin and keep you dry. This "wicking" layer can be long johns or light clothing made of a thin fabric, such as silk, Capilene polyester, hollow-core polyester, hydrophilic nylon, etc. For wicking away perspiration, Capilene is excellent.

Your second layer of clothing should act as insulation. Appropriate fabrics include some of the new synthetics, down, and wool. Wool is the traditional insulator, but it is not quite as good as newer fabrics when wet because it's heavy.

Your third layer should be windproof and waterproof. Gore-Tex is the most popular, waterproof, and breathable outdoor fabric, so many wildlife watchers use it. Other fabrics are equally waterproof but not so breathable, or vice-versa. For your windproof/waterproof layer, purchase a fabric that suits your primary activity best: buy something more waterproof for wet activities, more breathable for aerobic activities.

Don't forget to protect your extremities. Layer your gloves, too, or wear the type that wick, insulate, and repel wind and rain. And remember: dressing properly for warm weather is just as important as dressing for cold. In hot weather, consider the danger of sunstroke and overheating.

Optics

Binoculars and Spotting Scopes

A good pair of binoculars and a high-powered spotting scope are the two most important pieces of equipment a wildlife watcher can have. Binoculars and spotting scopes bridge the distance between you and a wild animal. You'll enjoy a better view while remaining a safe distance from wildlife, leaving animals undisturbed and keeping yourself safe.

Binoculars come in several sizes and degrees of magnification, such as 7 x 35, 8 x 40, and 10 x 50. The first number refers to how large the animal will be magnified compared to the naked eye. A "7x" figure, for example, means the animal is magnified seven times larger than it would be if you viewed it without binoculars. More magnification is not always better. Larger magnifications can amplify hand movements, making wildlife harder to see; a bird in a tree will be harder to find with a 10x magnification than with a 7x, because your small movements, even your breathing, will cause the image to move. The second number refers to the diameter of the large end of the lens (the end facing the animal). The greater that number, the greater the amount of light entering the lens—which means better viewing in dim light. A 7 x 50 pair of binoculars will produce an image approximately 1.5 times brighter than a 7 x 35 pair, though the 7 x 50 model will also be heavier. At one hundred feet, a 7 x 35 pair of binoculars will allow you to see an animal as if it were just fourteen feet away.

On some binoculars, you may notice a third number following the first two, expressed in degrees. This is the field of view that the binoculars cover (spotting scopes have a similar reading). The larger the field of view, the larger the area seen through the eyepiece.

There's no perfect pair of binoculars. When purchasing binoculars, consider in what conditions and circumstances they will be used, and choose accordingly. For example, pocket-size binoculars (such as size 8 x 21) are small and easy to carry. However, they do not work well in low light—but most animals are active in low light, and this is when the best wildlife viewing occurs. The most common size of binoculars chosen by wildlife watchers is 7 x 35; it strikes a reasonable balance between compact size and amount of light entering the lens.

Binoculars are relatively easy to use. First, locate the animal using your naked eye. Then bring the binoculars up to your eyes. If at first you don't succeed at finding your object in the lens, locate a larger object or landmark close to the animal with your naked eye. Make a mental note of where the animal is in relation to the large object. Bring the binoculars to your eyes again, find the larger object, then bring the animal into your field of vision.

Spotting scopes, which can be set on tripods, are used for viewing more stationary wildlife at long distances, such as animals tending a nest. Spotting scopes are monocular (having one lens) and feature much higher magnification than binoculars; you can see farther with them.

There are two types of
spotting scopes. Refractor
scopes are wide-angle, low-
magnification scopes for
viewing closer subjects. Catadioptric
scopes have a narrower field of view and
greater magnification. Catadioptric
scopes generally have lower-quality
resolution, so they are not as good
as refractor scopes for general use.

One of the best wildlife watching
memories I have is of watching nesting
bald eagles at Saint Marks National Wildlife
Refuge in Florida with a spotting scope. The scope was so powerful
I could see the eagle viewing me.

Night Vision Viewers

Originally designed for military and law enforcement use, night
vision viewers are used by wildlife viewers to open up a nocturnal
world and find previously unseen wildlife. Night vision viewers
monumentally enhance observation of such animals as bats, owls,
foxes, raccoons, and bears. Night goggles can provide some of the
greatest wildlife watching thrills.

Night vision viewers come in binocular and monocular forms,
and range in price from $400 for lower-quality Russian military
surplus products to more than $2,000 for higher-quality viewers. The
more expensive models reflect the latest optics
and electronics; some attachments have
zoom capabilities.

Be sure the viewer you select is water-
resistant, floats, and has the ability to resist
humidity and moisture, which can cause
internal fogging. Rupert Cutler, executive
director at Virginia's Explore Park in
Roanoke, has had staff lead nighttime wildlife

walks using night vision goggles for several years. Cutler points out that the same rules apply for nighttime watching as daytime watching: stay quiet and station yourself at a place frequented by wildlife.

Purchasing a night vision viewer is expensive; before you do so, study your options. Write away for information from various companies. One of the leaders in night vision viewers is ITT Night Vision, 7635 Plantation Road, Roanoke, VA 24019; phone (800) 448-8678.

Taking It to the Limit

The Iroquois National Wildlife Refuge in Alabama, New York, has taken wildlife watching with optics to new heights. Refuge officials have mounted two cameras in a bald eagle nesting tree; the cameras transmit live television pictures from the nest to a monitor in refuge headquarters. Eagles can be viewed during regular business hours. The birds lay their eggs in March; eaglets fledge in mid-July. For more information about this unique program, contact Iroquois National Wildlife Refuge, P.O. Box 517, 1101 Casey Road, Alabama, NY 14003; phone (716) 948-5445.

4 | Taking
to the
Field

No matter the time of day or time of year, North America always has wildlife to be observed, enjoyed, studied, and photographed. Fresh viewing opportunities arrive each day and each season, in every habitat and in every region. Some species, such as songbirds, ducks, hawks, and butterflies, are most active and best seen during the day. Others, such as owls, raccoons, bats, flying squirrels, and secretive bobcats, are most active at night.

Each hour brings diversity, and each season brings variety. Migrant songbirds arrive in spring from points south to nest and rear their young. Animals hidden all winter emerge from hibernation. In summer, when many of us take our vacations, deer feed in fields and teach their young to do the same. Fall means migration for many species;

for wildlife viewers, migration means unparalleled viewing opportunities. Wildlife viewing does not end with the arrival of winter. In fact, with the leaves off the trees, and wildlife in wintering grounds, winter can often be the best viewing season of all.

4 STEPS FOR SUCCESSFUL WILDLIFE VIEWING

I once entered Saint Marks National Wildlife Refuge in north Florida with hopes of seeing one of the many eagles that nest in the area. As I laced up my hiking boots at the Mounds Interpretive Trail, a very noisy group of people approached me. One young fellow was banging something and another young lady was talking at the top of her lungs. "Don't waste your time," one individual said, "There aren't any eagles back there."

Somewhat discouraged, I set out down the trail. Upon reaching one of my favorite spots, I sat to enjoy the wonderful view along the marsh, breathing in the salt air. Not five minutes later two bald eagles appeared in the distance and alighted, in plain view, on a snag about two hundred yards away. I set up my spotting scope and enjoyed one of the best eagle-watching days of my life—with the exception of slamming car doors, shouting, and shrieking in the distance as the group I had met in the parking lot made their grand exit.

Successful wildlife viewing doesn't just happen. You will greatly increase your chances of seeing wildlife by following some simple guidelines. Here are four basic steps for successful wildlife viewing:

1. *Look in the right place.*
2. *Look at the right time.*
3. *Develop wildlife viewing skills and techniques.*
4. *Understand the species and its habits.*

STEP ONE: LOOK IN THE RIGHT PLACE

If you want to see certain animals, you need to find out where—exactly—they live.

Each animal species is found only in a certain area, known as its range. White-tailed deer, for example, have a large range—you'll find them throughout most of the United States and southern Canada. Mule deer, on the other hand, live only in the western United States and southwest Canadian provinces—a smaller range. Black-tailed deer (a subspecies of mule deer) have a smaller range yet; they are found only in a narrow strip of woodlands and temperate coniferous forest along the Pacific Coast, from central California to Alaska.

An animal lives in a specific habitat within its range. A habitat is a place that provides the right combination of food, water, and cover a species needs for nesting, hiding, feeding, and sleeping. Habitat needs can vary greatly from one species to the next, even when the animals seem similar. Consider the red-tailed hawk and the red-shouldered hawk. To judge from their names, you might think these two birds are nearly identical. However, red-shouldered hawks prefer to live in swampy woods, where they feed mostly on snakes and frogs. Red-tailed hawks favor drier, open areas, such as fields and pasturelands, and feed mostly on small rodents. They prefer different habitats.

LIFE ON THE EDGE

Many animal species live on the edge.

An edge is any place where two different habitats meet, such as where a field meets a forest, or a pond meets cattails. Think of edges as transition zones where animals can feel safe. Deer and wild turkeys, for example, often feed in a field, but stay close to the forest where they can take cover if danger should appear.

Scan edge areas for wildlife. Look for standing dead trees: you'll have a good chance of seeing a hawk perched there, waiting for a rabbit or a mouse to enter the field.

Some species are extremely selective about habitat, while others can live in many places. For example, within their range (which includes most of North America), great horned owls can be found in a large number of different habitats, including forests, deserts, open country, and swamps. Great gray owls are much more selective within their northern range, living only in boreal coniferous forests and muskeg.

Most good field guides identify the preferred habitat of the animals you want to see. You can consult a field guide, then set out to locate that habitat on your next viewing trip. Recognizing the link between a species and its habitat is a fundamental lesson in successful wildlife viewing. It is also a lesson in wildlife conservation. Without its proper habitat, a wildlife species cannot exist. Habitat destruction and alteration are two of the greatest threats to North America's wildlife.

Here are examples of different habitats:

■ Open ocean
■ Seashore
■ Salt marsh

- Freshwater marsh
- Lakes, ponds, rivers
- Grassland
- Deciduous forest
- Coniferous forest

Here are some habitats with a few of the species you might see there:

- Old growth forest, Oregon
Spotted owl, pine marten, northern goshawk, northern flying squirrel.

- Sonoran Desert, Arizona
Desert bighorn sheep, javelina, large-eared kit fox, kangaroo rat, Gila woodpecker, elf owl, Gila monster, desert tortoise, zebra-tailed lizard.

■ Seashore, Assateague Island, Maryland–Virginia (summer)
Brown pelican, sanderling, semipalmated sandpiper, black skimmer, several species of gull (laughing, ring-billed, herring, and greater black-backed).

The link between habitats and wildlife can be illustrated with a hypothetical summer hike through a conifer forest in central New York. The hike meanders through various plant communities, and each community offers different wildlife viewing opportunities. The trail begins in a grassy area, then winds through low shrubs, and eventually goes through high shrubs. The high shrubs give way to a shrub-tree community, then the trail enters an opening. The trail then moves into an area of low trees. As the trail moves deeper into the forest, the trees get taller. The trail ends in a mature forest.

While we are lacing up our hiking boots in the early morning in the grassy area, a high pitched "kip-kip-kip" catches our attention. It is the song of the diminutive grasshopper sparrow. Looking back down at our boots, we are distracted by motion; we see a meadow jumping mouse scurrying for cover. Hiking toward the forest, we enter the shrub area where we observe a purple finch and listen to a song sparrow. Hiking away from the shrubby area and into the opening, we spot a white-tailed deer browsing. We cross into the low tree community and spot a Nashville warbler. Finally, in the mature forest, while we take a break on a fallen log, a veery—a tawny-colored thrush—flies by.

Each of these animals prefers a different kind of habitat. We would not likely have seen a veery in the grassy area where the hike began. And since the grasshopper sparrow likes open grassy and weedy meadows, it would probably not have been in the mature forest at trail's end. Some species might live in several of the natural communities along the trail. We might have seen an Eastern cottontail rabbit in the grassy areas, the shrub community, and in the forest opening, but it wouldn't be found in mature forest. We would not have observed red squirrels at the beginning of the hike, but might have watched them leap from tree to tree at the walk's end.

Elevation also plays an important role in wildlife viewing. Habitat and climate change with increasing elevation, affecting the wildlife community. The mammal population changes within several elevation

THERE'S LIFE IN THAT DEAD TREE

One of the best places to search for wildlife is in and around a snag.

A snag is a standing dead tree. Think of snags as animal condominiums. Hawks and eagles use snags because their few branches and no leaves provide prime vantage points for hunting prey. Cavity-nesting birds such as woodpeckers excavate holes in the decaying wood. Flying squirrels, nuthatches, bluebirds, bats, owls, and American kestrels use cavities abandoned by other animals, or make nests in natural holes that result from lost branches or lightning strikes. Squirrels use snags as a place to store food; insect-eating birds search for prey there.

There is life, and lots of it, in that dead tree.

zones and, with it, so do mammal viewing opportunities at Yosemite National Park in California. Here's an overview of where in Yosemite some mammals live:

■ Foothills: 500 to 3,000 feet
Western harvest mouse, dusky-footed wood rat, spotted skunk, mule deer, bobcat.

■ Lower montane: 3,000 to 6,000 feet
Deer mouse, California ground squirrel, western gray squirrel, California mole, valley pocket gopher, mink, ringtail, coyote, bobcat, mule deer, mountain lion, black bear.

■ Upper montane: 6,000 to 8,000 feet
Lodgepole chipmunk, bush-tailed wood rat, Douglas squirrel, northern flying squirrel, golden-mantled ground squirrel, yellow-bellied marmot, porcupine, long-tailed weasel, river otter, coyote, mule deer, black bear.

■ Subalpine: 8,000 to 11,000 feet
Water shrew, heather vole, belding ground squirrel, pika, mountain pocket gopher, mule deer (summer), bighorn sheep.

■ Alpine: 11,000 feet and above
Alpine chipmunk, alpine gopher, pika.

STEP TWO: LOOK AT THE RIGHT TIME

Timing is everything. Animal activity depends on the time of day and the time of year.

Some animals, such as songbirds, hawks, and red and gray squirrels, are active during the day (diurnal). Other species, such as owls, bats, raccoons, bobcats, flying squirrels, and opossums are active at night (nocturnal). In general, early morning and evening are the best times to view most birds and large mammals, since they are most active at these times. At midday, watch for hawks "kettling," circling and soaring on columns of rising warm air. Most amphibians and reptiles are active at night for three reasons. First, their prey—insects—are more active and plentiful then. Second, harsh sun rays can dry out reptiles' porous skin, such as that of salamanders. And third, darkness affords greater protection from predators.

Some wildlife species are present in particular areas only during certain times of the year. If you want to see the 7,500 elk at the National Elk Refuge in Jackson, Wyoming, go there in winter. If you visit in summer, those same elk will be in the high country, miles away.

Want to see bald eagles? Lots of bald eagles? Timing is everything. One of the largest concentrations of bald eagles in the lower forty-eight states occurs in winter at the Klamath Basin along the Oregon–California border. Most of the eagles there come from Canada for the winter, arriving in November and departing by April. More than five hundred eagles are present during January and February. For more information about this fine eagle site, contact Klamath Basin National Wildlife Refuge, Route 1, Box 74, Tule Lake, CA 96134;

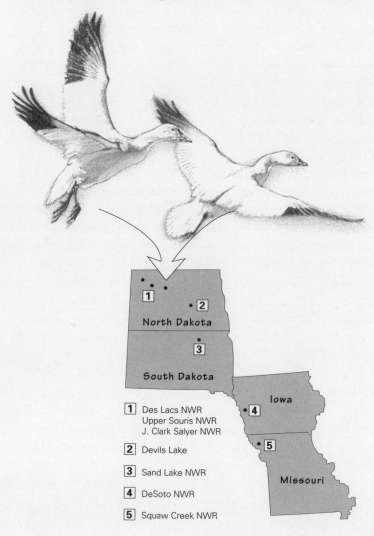

North Dakota

1

2

South Dakota

3

Iowa

1 Des Lacs NWR
Upper Souris NWR
J. Clark Salyer NWR

4

2 Devils Lake

3 Sand Lake NWR

5

4 DeSoto NWR

Missouri

5 Squaw Creek NWR

phone (916) 667-2231. Or contact the Oregon Department of Fish and Wildlife, 1400 Miller Island Road, West Klamath Falls, OR 97603; phone (503) 883-5732.

Timing really matters if you want to witness spectacular wildlife displays during spring and fall migrations. Here's an example of how the timing of migration relates to viewing snow geese in the central United States (see map, opposite page): at Squaw Creek National Wildlife Refuge in northwestern Missouri, gatherings of up to 300,000 snow geese have been observed during their fall

"There is a direct correlation between seeing wildlife and spending enough time in the field."

-*Mark Hilliard*
Watchable Wildlife Coordinator
Bureau of Land Management

migration in October and November. Where did all of these geese come from? Most of the snow geese seen at Squaw Creek spend summers breeding and raising young along the west coast of the Hudson Bay. Between August and October, as the arctic summer comes to a close, the geese begin migrating south in flocks of 100 to 1,000. They fly between forty and fifty miles per hour at altitudes of around 3,000 feet (although they have been recorded as high as 20,000 feet). Some of these birds fly nonstop to wintering grounds on the Gulf Coast or Mexico, but other flocks stop along the way.

Some of the first stops are the Des Lacs, Upper Souris, and J. Clark Salyer national wildlife refuges in northwest North Dakota. When inclement weather drives the geese from these areas, they continue south to Devils Lake Wetland Management District in east-central North Dakota, then go still farther south to Sand Lake, South Dakota. When cold drives the geese from Sand Lake, they move on to DeSoto National Wildlife Refuge in Iowa, then fly to Squaw Creek. As winter tightens its grip and the marshes at Squaw Creek freeze, the snow geese move again, this time to their wintering grounds along the Gulf Coast of Texas and Louisiana.

Here today, gone next week, or perhaps the week after.

For more information on the snow geese migration, contact Squaw Creek National Wildlife Refuge, P.O. Box 101, Mound City, MO 64470; phone (816) 442-3187.

Other Timing Issues to Consider

Hibernation

Some animals appear only at certain times of the year, but not because they migrate. These animals are sometimes out of sight because they hibernate, or become inactive during the winter season. The Columbian ground squirrels of Glacier National Park, for instance, are active and visible for only about five months of the year. Emerging from hibernation in April, they begin immediate preparations for the next winter, feeding on grasses, seeds, and other vegetation. They disappear by August or September and will hibernate for the next seven to eight months.

Tides

Tides affect wildlife viewing success. Most shorebirds and whales are best observed at high tides, while intertidal life can be explored during low tides.

Weather

Changes in weather can present wildlife viewing opportunities. After rain, many predators emerge to feed on displaced insects and rodents. Wetter, cooler weather associated with low-pressure systems can increase your chance of seeing animals. Many animals are active just after a storm, and wildlife seems less sensitive to noise and smell at that time.

The best time to view Florida manatees is in winter right after a cold front, when the manatees gather around the warm-water discharges of power plants and congregate at warm springs, such as those found in Kings Bay–Crystal River National Wildlife Refuge and Homosassa Springs State Wildlife Park.

Cold fronts often "push" migrating birds south in the fall. On September 14, 1978, more than 21,000 broad-winged hawks were spotted in one day over Hawk Mountain, Pennsylvania, as a massive cold front came down from Canada. The best viewing of bald eagles on the Upper Mississippi River National Wildlife and Fish Refuge in Winona, Minnesota, "occurs after periods of bitter weather, when

ORNITHOLOGY 101

Ornithology—the study of birds—is one of the more difficult courses wildlife management students must pass to earn a degree. Students must identify hundreds of birds, learn dozens of bird songs, and memorize numerous scientific names. Such stress gives rise to a good number of amusing stories about ornithology courses.

One of the best stories I know involved a group of budding wildlife managers eager to take a midsemester exam focusing on bird identification. The well-prepared students walked into the classroom only to find all the mounted bird specimens covered with towels. Only the birds' feet were visible.

"What is this?" asked one startled student.

"What's going on here?" asked another.

Smiling, the professor explained that to be a truly outstanding ornithologist, one had to be able to identify birds using only the shapes of their feet. A silence fell upon the students, until one frustrated individual stood up and said, "This is ridiculous . . . I'm leaving."

As the student walked toward the door, the professor bolted up to confront him. "You can't leave my classroom."

"Oh, yes I can," replied the student, "just watch me."

"Okay, okay," said the professor, "but before you leave, you must tell me your name. I do not believe I know your name."

The frustration on the student's face turned quickly to a grin. He reached down, grabbed his foot with one hand and pointed at it with the other, all the while staring at the professor.

"You tell me what my name is, sir. You tell me."

alternative fishing areas in the backwaters are frozen and eagles concentrate along the main channel," notes Henry Schneider of the refuge. The city of Wabasha, Minnesota, has an observation deck staffed with Eagle Watch volunteers on weekends from November until March. Call the Winona, Minnesota, Convention and Visitors Bureau at (800) 657-4972 for more information on eagle and swan watch tours.

Staging

A magnificent birding time is during staging, when large flocks of migrating birds gather in a concentrated area to feed, rest, or wait out bad weather. Places like Cape May in New Jersey and Fisherman Island National Wildlife Refuge, Virginia, can offer phenomenal viewing of staging birds. Fisherman Island has hosted millions of passerines such as eastern bluebirds, eastern meadowlarks, and tree swallows during fall migration. In November at Riecks Lake Park, north of Alma, Wisconsin, tundra swans stage until freeze-up before continuing their journey to the East Coast.

STEP THREE: DEVELOP WILDLIFE VIEWING SKILLS AND TECHNIQUES

Wildlife is often closer and more abundant than you might think. Developing sharp senses is the first step to seeing more animals in the field. While looking for wildlife, make it a game to really focus your eyes and tune your ears. Most animals camouflage themselves, blending into the environment, so you'll need to look at more than the obvious. Try the following:

■ Look for subtle movements in bushes, shrubs, and trees.
■ Make "owl eyes"—make an "okay" sign with your hand, bring the rest of your fingers into the circle, then look through them. This helps focus your attention.
■ Look for parts of an animal, rather than its entire body.

Some additional suggestions from the National Partners in Watchable Wildlife brochure, "Ultimate Guide to Wildlife Watching," include:

■ Make "mule ears"—cup your hands over your ears to amplify natural sounds.

■ Look above and below you. Animals occupy niches in all the vertical and horizontal layers of a habitat. Don't just look directly in front of you; look up and down, too.

■ Heed your instincts. If the hair on the back of your neck stands up, an animal may be near.

■ Relax your muscles. Animals can easily detect tension.

■ Look for out-of-place shapes, such as horizontal shapes in a mostly vertical forest, or an oblong shape on a linear tree branch.

■ Focus and expand your attention, taking in the foreground and then switching to take in the wide view.

■ Use your peripheral vision rather than turning your head.

The animal you are watching most likely considers you a predator. Take yourself out of that role. The following tricks can help:

■ Avoid sudden movements. Many animals will tolerate observation if no quick motions or loud noises are made.

■ Do not try to sneak up on animals. It probably won't work and you may place yourself in danger.

■ Do not stare at animals. Wear a hat that conceals your eyes.

Strategies

Use these strategies to get close to wildlife:

■ Use optics.
■ Use a vehicle as a blind.
■ Hide behind a blind.
■ Sit still.
■ Walk quietly and slowly.
■ Place decoys.
■ Mask or wear scents.
■ Set bait.

- Imitate calls.
- Use special lights.
- Hire a professional guide.
- Go on guided outings.

Optics

As already noted, using binoculars and spotting scopes are the two best ways to get close to wildlife. (See page 41 for more on selecting and using optics.)

Using a Vehicle as a Blind

Vehicles make excellent blinds, even though this method is certainly not as cool or as glitzy as other wildlife viewing techniques. Many animals have become habituated to vehicles; they don't seem to be afraid of them and will often approach or pass right by your car. Turn your engine off, sit quietly in your vehicle and wait for wildlife to come to you. If you need to shift around inside your vehicle, move slowly. Do not get out when animals are near—you'll send them off in an acute panic. If you see animals while your car is running, don't turn the engine off, since this will also panic them.

Blinds

A blind is anything that conceals you from the animals you want to observe. Blinds may include your vehicle, boxes, homemade blinds, even fancy, portable, commercial blinds similar to a pop-up tent. Some modern blinds actually roll out over your body from a helmet, popping over you from a backpacklike frame.

Blinds are used because some animals, such as waterfowl, have excellent eyesight, and blinds conceal your movement. Place blinds upwind, and have the sun to your back, so the animal will have to look into the sun in order to see you. Don't set up blinds in the midst of wildlife. Blinds do not give you the right to get too close.

The Medicine Lake National Wildlife Refuge in Medicine Lake, Montana, provides a sharp-tailed grouse photo blind that can be reserved on a first-come, first-served basis. The blind is erected near a busy dancing ground in mid-April and is removed once the grouse have completed their breeding displays, according to Robert Romero, refuge operations specialist. From the blind, photographers and wildlife viewers are treated to a view of the elaborate courtship ritual—strutting and stomping—of male sharp-tailed grouse. To reserve the blind, contact Medicine Lake National Wildlife Refuge, 223 North Lake Shore Road, Medicine Lake, MT 59247-9600; phone (406) 789-2305.

Lostwood National Wildlife Refuge also maintains a blind for watching male grouse attempt to woo their females, and boasts one of the highest populations of sharp-tailed grouse in the nation. Contact Lostwood National Wildlife Refuge, Rural Route 2, Box 98, Kenmare, ND 58746; phone (701) 848-2722.

Sitting Still

Find a comfortable place, sit down, relax, and remain still. Most animals' eyes are made to detect motion. Lean up against a tree to break your silhouette. Trees and vegetation make great viewing blinds. If you wear dark-colored clothes or camouflage and use a dropcloth of camouflage netting, you'll increase the odds of going unnoticed. If you sit absolutely still, you will also see animals reappear because they'll think you have gone.

Sitting aloof may also help. Act disinterested. Look around slowly and not directly at animals.

wind direction

Walk Quietly and Slowly

Few animals walk with the steady gait that humans do. Break your natural pattern: take a few steps, avoiding brittle sticks or leaves, then stop, look, and listen.

Walk into the wind whenever possible, since many animals have an excellent sense of smell (see illustration on opposite page). Bob Hernbrode of the Colorado Division of Wildlife suggests that if you cross rivers or streams, you should "look upstream and downstream. Often the sound of the flowing water will deaden your noise and the animal will not realize you are close." Or take a roundabout route, and consider your silhouette.

Do not approach any animal directly—act disinterested. Look all around you, and again, do not stare at the animal. If that bird or deer you are moving toward appears nervous or skittish, stop until it feels comfortable. If you begin to approach again and the animal still appears nervous or skittish, you are too close. From here, break out your binoculars and watch from the distance where the animal is comfortable.

How close is too close? In Yellowstone National Park, approaching on foot within one hundred yards of any wildlife—or within any distance that disturbs or displaces wildlife—is strictly prohibited.

Decoys

According to archeological research, Native Americans used decoys more than two thousand years ago, crafting them from tule reeds, cattails, twine, feathers, and mineral paint. A decoy lures an animal within range for a better view or photograph. To wild animals, decoys represent companionship and safety, and point to a feeding and resting area.

Decoys are often used in conjunction with blinds. Some successful waterfowl decoys are much, much larger than real birds. And hunters have discovered that decoys need not be lifelike. Snow geese, for example, will decoy to pieces of sheet or white plastic bleach bottles.

Decoys have been used to lure ducks, geese, shorebirds, pronghorn antelope, deer, elk, sandhill cranes, blue herons, and wild turkeys. Some seasoned wildlife watchers place a heron or crane silhouette near their blinds as a "confidence builder" for other species; the sight of these long-legged, wary birds can convince ducks or geese that an area is safe.

Positioning decoys is an art, as any waterfowl hunter will tell you. For example, relaxed ducks that are feeding tend to spread themselves out. If your decoys are all bunched up, real ducks may interpret them as a nervous flock about to depart.

Scents

There are two types of scents: attracting scents and cover scents.

Attracting scents pull animals to you. These scents include such aromatic delicacies as urine of fox, rabbit, deer, or elk, as well as apples, bacon drippings, or fish. Place these upwind of your blind.

Cover scents mask your scent. Bob Hernbrode explains that cover scents are usually placed a few feet or yards downwind from a blind. "Skunk is the most common and effective of these cover scents," he says, "although others such as apples or sage are also used. Scents are usually applied to a cotton ball hung from a string, or placed on the ground—they may also be used on your person, on a sleeve, hat, or shoes, to cover your own scent as you move around."

Baiting

Baiting is the use of food to attract wildlife. Although a few wildlife watchers use baiting, most wildlife professionals do not support the practice. It is highly artificial as well as strictly regulated in many areas. Limit baiting to your backyard birdfeeder.

Calls

Many animals can be "called in" with the use of sounds. Coyotes, foxes, bobcats, squirrels, deer, elk, moose, antelope, pheasants, wild turkeys, waterfowl, and many songbirds will respond to calls. To make a wildlife call, do the following:

■ Loudly whisper "psh" or "hiss" into your hand. This will call in songbirds such as nuthatches and chickadees.
■ Kiss the back of your hand to create a higher-pitched squealing sound. This will bring in many birds and small mammals.

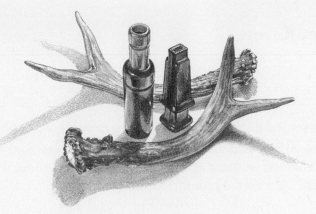

■ Rattle deer or elk antlers on a fall afternoon. This can attract rutting deer.

■ Play tape recordings of animal sounds. The recorded squeals of a dying rabbit can bring in owls.

Calling animals with recordings is controversial. Limit calls to common species; use calls only during times of the year when it will not distress the animal. Never use calls or recordings for rare or endangered species of wildlife. Taped calls are prohibited in many areas, so check with the site manager before you use calls. When in doubt, don't.

Montana forester and photographer Bill Gabriel notes that in some areas, tape recorders can be detrimental to wildlife. "People playing recordings under a nesting tree caused some common black hawks to abandon the Sonoita Creek Sanctuary in Arizona, and some of the few elegant trogons in the United States were harassed out of Arizona's Cave Creek Canyon by people with tape players." Bill offers the following dos and don'ts for using a tape recorder:

■ DO take time to learn the songs and call notes of the species you are interested in pursuing.

■ DON'T use territorial songs unless you first hear a singing bird.

■ DO play the call only a few times. If no bird responds, move on and try another area.

■ DO turn off the tape as soon as the bird responds.

■ DON'T use tapes in areas where few people visit a few special birds.

■ DO keep the volume at a minimum. More is not better.

DIFFERENCES? WHAT DIFFERENCES?

While I was a graduate student at Yale, I had the opportunity to study under Dr. Stephen Kellert, world-renowned for his pioneering work in understanding public attitudes toward wildlife. After graduating, I started my career as a wildlife biologist with the Florida Game and Fresh Water Fish Commission. One of my first assignments was a public speaking engagement with a raccoon hunting club in north Florida.

Eager to share what I had learned while working with Dr. Kellert, I talked about public attitudes toward wildlife. I asserted that when it comes to people and their views of wildlife, there is no such thing as a "general public." People who live in rural areas think about wildlife differently than people who live in urban or suburban areas, I said. Older citizens think differently about wildlife than do people who are twenty-five to forty years old. Women think differently than men.

A rather large raccoon hunter stood up in the back of the room, totally unimpressed with my lecture thus far. "Boy, are you married?" he asked.

"Yes sir," I replied cautiously, wondering where this was leading.

He continued, "Well, it doesn't take no research project from Yale to tell me that men and women think differently, now, does it?"

Lights

Many animals cannot see red light; to them, it just looks black. Some wildlife watchers use red beams in conjunction with blinds at night to view nocturnal creatures.

Hiring a Guide

Don't be afraid to look for experienced hunting or fishing guides to help you make the most of a wildlife viewing trip. More and more hunting and fishing guides are being hired by wildlife viewers. Guides know the area and the tricks of the trade, such as how to place decoys, call in turkeys and ducks, and find wildlife.

On Maryland's Eastern Shore, traditional waterfowl hunting guides take out more and more wildlife watchers each year. Though guides are expensive, their expertise is usually worth the money. With a guide, it's possible to learn in an afternoon what would take you a month or more to figure out on your own.

Guided Outings

Most parks and refuges offer nature and wildlife walks, and many local Audubon groups and other wildlife organizations offer outings guided by professionals. There's no better way to learn about wildlife than from people who have made wildlife management their profession.

STEP FOUR: UNDERSTAND THE SPECIES AND ITS HABITS

When viewing an animal, observe its colors, shape, "field marks," and behavior. Hone your skills in identifying different species, and notice the differences between male and female animals, and between younger animals and older ones. For example, although the Kentucky warbler and the common yellowthroat look somewhat similar, the Kentucky warbler has distinctive yellow patches, like spectacles, around its eyes. Female belted kingfishers have brown breastbands while males do not. Juvenile bald eagles lack the distinctive white head and tail so characteristic of adult birds.

Wildlife Identification

Identifying wildlife is a lifelong process. Nothing will help you more than a good set of field guides to go with your binoculars. Start off by identifying the animal as a mammal, bird, fish, reptile, amphibian, or insect. Then ask yourself the following questions:

What is the animal's size?
Size makes a difference. Beavers and muskrats are both aquatic

mammals, but once you learn a few key characteristics you can easily tell one from the other. The beaver has a broad, hairless, paddle-shaped tail; the muskrat's tail is thin and ropelike. Beavers grow much larger than muskrats. An adult beaver weighs between thirty and sixty pounds, while an adult muskrat weighs between two and four pounds.

What is the animal's color?

Color helps distinguish between species and between sexes. Male ducks, known as *drakes*, are brightly colored in the spring. Some animals change color for winter, such as the snowshoe or varying hare. Short-tailed weasels shed brown summer coats for white winter ones. The white-tailed ptarmigan, found in some mountainous areas of the West, changes its plumage from pure white in winter to a mottled gray, brown, and white in summer.

What is the animal's shape?

Observe the beak of a red-tailed hawk. It's hooked and stout and perfect for tearing flesh. Now notice the bill of a blue-winged teal. It's flat and fairly long, and is used to strain tiny animals from the water. Paying attention to the shape of an animal's features can help in identification. For instance, white-tailed deer antlers have a main

beam with tines branching from it; a mule deer's antlers branch more uniformly. Bald and golden eagles fly with flattened wings, unlike vultures, which soar with their wings in a "V," and ospreys, which fly with wings that appear bent.

What type of habitat is the animal in?

The red fox prefers open fields, meadows, and edge habitats whereas the gray fox prefers more wooded areas, as illustrated below.

Is the animal vocalizing?

Green tree frogs "queenk," southern leopard frogs give three to five "croaks" followed by two or three "clucks," and bullfrogs call "jug-o'-rum." Great horned owls hoot, "Hoo, hoo-oo, hoo, hoo"; barred owls call, "Hoohoo-hoohoo, hoohoo-hoohooaw"; and great gray owls sing, "Whoo-hoo-hoo."

What is the animal doing?

Specific activities can often give important clues for identification. Dabbling ducks feed by doing a sort of headstand, tipping their rumps in the air as they probe for grasses and the seeds of underwater plants. Dabbling ducks can take flight from the water directly into the air.

EXPERIENCED SNAKE HANDLER; DON'T TRY THIS AT HOME

While living in Tallahassee, Florida, I had the opportunity to take a field ecology course at Florida State University with one of the best field biologists in the nation, Dr. Bruce Means. Dr. Means seems to be an authority on every animal that moves, but he is renowned for his work with rattlesnakes.

On one of many field trips, our class took a respite from the midday Florida sun and went swimming in a cool, crystalline spring in Apalachicola National Forest. Quite hungry after swimming, we began hiking back to the van for lunch, stepping more quickly as we became hungrier and hungrier.

I took off running, yelling to my teacher that I would beat him back to the van. Pounding along the fire road, I leaped over a large branch. Only in midair did I realize that it wasn't a branch at all, but the largest eastern diamondback rattlesnake I had ever seen, stretched completely across the road, sunning itself. I caught my footing and turned to warn the others.

Any sane individual, upon seeing this five-foot-long reptile, would have stepped back in amazement. But, without hesitation, and clad only in his swimsuit, Dr. Means reached down with both hands and PICKED UP THE SNAKE. Johnny Weissmuller's Tarzan movies may have been filmed at Wakulla Springs, not ten miles away, but I was witnessing a real-life Tarzan! So much for the professor in the ivory tower. This was real-world Biology 101.

One by one we examined the monstrous rattlesnake writhing in our professor's hands. Then Dr. Means walked calmly over to the side of the fire road and released it. "Wouldn't want anyone to step on him," he commented, quickly adding, "Class dismissed."

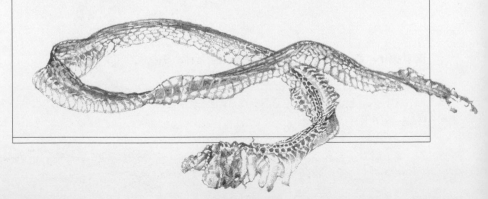

Diving or sea ducks dive completely underwater to feed on small fish, crustaceans, mollusks, and aquatic plants. These ducks must run or patter along the top of the water to build up speed before taking flight.

Is the animal found in this region? This habitat?

Once you are reasonably sure you have identified the animal you are watching, consult your field guide's section on the species' range and habitat to make sure it lives in the area in which you have found it.

Animal Behavior

Don't just look at wildlife—learn to observe it. What is the animal doing? Resting? Feeding? Try to understand what you are seeing and hearing. What might look like random behavior is actually the animal performing an important survival function. Here are some examples:

■ Shorebirds use their bills to "feel" for food. Highly sensitive and specialized nerve endings in their bills enable shorebirds to seize crustaceans in the sand. Watch them probe for snails, clams, and worms. Observe how the different bill lengths are related to the foods each species eats.

■ The yellow-bellied sapsucker pokes holes around the trunk of a tree, not to eat animals in the bark but to allow sap to ooze out. Insects become stranded in the sap, providing this resourceful bird with a meal.

■ In Badlands National Park, visitors often wonder why bison take dust baths in the loose dirt of prairie dog towns. The coating of dust helps protect bison from pesky insects.

Wildlife Calling Cards: Tracks and Signs

You don't always have to see wildlife to enjoy wildlife. Animals often leave clues about their movements and daily routines. Among these are the following:

TRACK TRAPS

*T*ry "trapping" tracks by smoothing over sand or mud (preferably near water) and returning the next day to see what may have walked by. The tracks shown here belong to deer.

■ Owl pellets. Owls cannot digest the fur and bones of the small mammals they eat. These lovely leftovers are regurgitated in pellet form. Look for them around the bases of large trees. If you find pellets, you're probably standing beneath an owl's home base.

■ Whitewash. Look for "whitewash" (droppings) on cliffs or beneath trees. This indicates the presence of a roost, nest, or colony of birds.

■ Game trails. These narrow trails mark routes to food, shelter, or water.

■ Fur/hair. You may find fur or hair along the edges of the entrance to a den tree or on a fence where animals have passed. Inspect the fur. What color is it?

■ Deer rubs. Look for marks on trees from antler rubbing or gnawing.

■ Dead birds. These are often the remains of a predator's meal.

■ Browse lines. Look for leafless areas in shrubs and stands of young trees. These are caused by too many feeding deer in an area.

■ Woodpecker signs. Rows of small holes encircling live trees are signs of yellow-bellied sapsuckers.

■ Bird nests. Nests come in all shapes and sizes. Early spring, prior to green-up, is a great time to see and inspect nests of previous years. Can you associate a particular nest with the bird that made it?

■ Flattened grass. Tamped grass in a field or clearing tells you that an animal has bedded down there.

■ Scat—okay, animal poop. Scat can be identified by its contents. Black bear scat is soft and dark in the fall but resembles horse manure in summer. Mountain lion scat looks like large domestic cat scat.

■ Rises. When trout and other fish species feed in a lake or stream, they make small dimples, or rises, on the surface of the water as they tip upward to eat insects or other aquatic life.

■ Tracks. Look for animal tracks in snow, in loose dirt, in soft ground, or near water. Bears, skunks, beavers, porcupines, and raccoons walk flatfooted. Wolves, foxes, coyotes, mountain lions, and bobcats walk on their toes. Deer, elk, moose, pronghorn, mountain sheep, and mountain goats walk on their toenails or hooves.

■ Shoreline clues. Notice stick and mud dams across streams; large conical houses of mud and sticks at the edge of a lake; pointed tree stumps near water. Any or all of these signs will tell you that beavers live in the area.

■ Sounds. Listen for the characteristic "slap" of water as a beaver dives below the surface; the sound is made by the beaver's tail striking the water and serves as a warning for others of potential danger.

Wildlife Management

Most of the wildlife you view lives partly as the result of work by wildlife management professionals. While in the field, you may notice some of the following management techniques:

Water Control

On many national wildlife refuges and state waterfowl-wetland management areas, water control is one of the most important management tools. Managers construct dikes and create shallow impoundments for wildlife. Water in marshes is drained in spring, stimulating plant growth and thus providing food for ducks and geese. In fall, marshes are flooded again to make seeds available to waterfowl. At Trustom Pond Refuge in Rhode Island, wildlife managers lower water levels by opening breachways to the ocean. This practice exposes mudflats, which become feeding areas for shorebirds and nesting islands for common terns.

Controlled Burning

Periodic regulated burning of many ecosystems, including grasslands and some forests, is essential for maintaining productive wildlife habitat. In the Florida Keys, the U.S. Fish and Wildlife Service burns woody undergrowth. This stimulates the growth of tender shoots, providing food for the diminutive Key deer. In Congaree Swamp National Monument in South Carolina, park managers set prescribed burns to maintain critical nesting habitat for the federally listed endangered red-cockaded woodpecker.

Nest Boxes and Platforms

Nest boxes are common sights in wildlife viewing areas. Placed along field edges, small nest boxes are designed to attract bluebirds and provide homes where there is a shortage of natural cavities. These boxes are usually about five feet above ground and have an entrance hole that is one-half to one inch in diameter. Larger wood duck boxes are placed in wetland areas. Metal guards are placed below these boxes to keep out predators such as raccoons and snakes.

Nesting platforms for ospreys are generally built eight to ten feet (or higher) above open water. Nesting platforms for Canada geese are only a foot or two above open shallow water or on the edge of a marsh.

Plantings

In the prairie pothole region, wildlife managers plant native grasses to provide nesting cover for waterfowl. At Eufaula National Wildlife Refuge in Alabama, they plant large tracts of winter grain, such as soybeans, peanuts, millet, corn, and sorghum. These crops are used by waterfowl during winter.

Seasonal Closures

Many parks and refuges close certain areas to visitors to protect sensitive wildlife during critical times of the year. In winter, wildlife managers in the West close certain trails to snowmobilers to protect mule deer and elk; these animals are already stressed due to limited availability of forage. Shorebirds are particularly sensitive to human intrusion while nesting, so prohibiting entry to shorebird nesting areas is critical for nesting success.

Fortunately, most people agree with this wildlife management practice. In a public opinion study I conducted for the Georgia Wildlife Resources Division, 86 percent of respondents moderately or strongly supported limiting public access to certain fish and wildlife management areas to protect sensitive wildlife.

Law Enforcement

Wildlife managers must also enforce the law. Law enforcement is an important management tool, since it curbs poaching and fosters appropriate interactions with wildlife.

It's also a dangerous part of the job. My consulting work has taken me to nearly every state fish and wildlife agency in the nation at one time or another; I don't know of one office that does not have a plaque on its walls memorializing a wildlife officer killed in the line of duty.

Wildlife Population Monitoring

At a viewing site, you might get lucky and see biologists banding, trapping, or releasing wild animals. Bird banding and census-taking of wildlife populations are two methods employed by biologists to measure the health of animal populations.

Mowing

Mown areas on refuges or in wildlife management areas maintain open habitat for wildlife such as the American woodcock, bobwhite quail, and whitetail deer.

FEELING LUCKY? NOT SO FAMOUS BEAR STORIES

One of the thrills of wildlife watching is that you can never be sure exactly when you will see wildlife. Sometimes it takes days to see what you are after. Other times wildlife reveals itself unexpectedly. Be prepared for both.

As a high school student I spent many weekends backpacking in Shenandoah National Park with Jim Omans, now a forester with the Department of Defense. One exceptionally dark night we set up camp in White Oak Canyon, a beautiful gorge noted for its many waterfalls and virgin hemlock stands.

In the middle of the night I was awakened by a ripping sound—the sound of a raccoon ripping up my brand-new backpack. It seemed strange that a raccoon would be able to reach our packs, since Jim and I had hung them from a tree to elude the many marauding black bears in the area. Clad only in underwear and untied hiking boots, I went over to shoo the raccoon away.

➤

Stumbling through pitch darkness toward the sound of continuous ripping, I reached the packs and was surprised at how low they were now hanging. "Oh well," I said to myself, "my knot must have slipped." I began to shove at the pack, believing the raccoon would startle and run for cover. This particular raccoon seemed to be quite large, probably due to all the free lunches it was getting from campers. But I wasn't deterred; it wasn't going to get any more of my food.

I pushed again. Then my flashlight slipped and the beam illuminated the ground, where a very large raccoon labored on, shredding my pack—only I saw now that it wasn't a raccoon at all, but a fairly large black bear, now face-to-face with me!

I pushed myself back, stumbling to the ground. Jim came over and we began yelling to scare the bear away. But the bear showed little concern over a future wildlife biologist and a forester in their underwear and untied hiking boots. It continued to enjoy a freeze-dried beef stroganoff dinner.

This was not the last of my unexpected bouts with bears. Shortly after I was married, my wife Mary Anne and I journeyed to the Great Smoky Mountains National Park to hike and view wildlife. I was well-acquainted with the park, having worked there for two summers as a teenager, and I knew one of the best places in the park to see bears was Mount LeConte. Citing many facts on black bear ecology and biology, I impressed my bride with my knowledge of bears. Except—the bears never showed.

After a long day of hiking we set up for a snack on a rocky outcropping atop Mount LeConte, complete with a 150-foot cliff and a spectacular view. We were enjoying the scenery when Mary Anne caught sight of a black bear. "Keep still," I said, "we'll get a better view."

A better view we did get, as the bear ambled slowly toward us. Pleased with our good luck, I glanced back out over the cliff to enjoy the view. Then it hit me: we were sandwiched between a 250-pound bear and a 150-foot cliff. My wife, confident of the situation—she was accompanied by a bear expert after all— enjoyed the experience, even remarking, "Here we are with a cliff behind us and a bear in front of us."

"Yeah," I slowly replied.

Luckily the bear lost interest in us and soon left the area (as I'd predicted he would).

Encountering the animals you set out to see can be a real challenge. Before a trip to Denali National Park in Alaska, I had never observed a grizzly bear in the wild. Thrilled at the possibility, I made plans and collected information. "What time of day is best to see grizzlies?" I asked. "What areas are best to see one? Have any grizzlies been spotted within the past few days?" After several unsuccessful forays into the park, I came to the disappointing conclusion that I would have to wait to see a grizzly.

The day of our departure, I decided to try one last time.

➤ "The train back to Anchorage won't wait for us," my wife reminded me. But I had to try again. It might be several years before I returned. I spent several hours touring an area known to have occasional grizzly sightings. Again I was disappointed, and found little consolation in the wise words I had often given to novice viewers—the theory that so much wildlife viewing happens by chance.

And then chance paid me a visit. Seemingly out of nowhere, a very blonde, very large grizzly appeared, walking slowly up a streambed. My first thought was that my wife would not believe me when I told her—she had accompanied me on my previous excursions. My second thought was that, for the first time during the trip, I did not have my camera at my side. But there it was.

The female bear, called a sow, walked slowly up the streambed in plain view three hundred yards away. I noted the distinct hump above her shoulders, her very large size, and her coloration; she was so blonde she was nearly pale yellow. I followed her through my binoculars for close to fifteen minutes, savoring the view and my good fortune. Then I quickly traveled back to the lodge where my wife and daughter were in line for the shuttle bus and anxiously awaiting my return. Luckily, the bus was late, and I was able to catch the train back to Anchorage.

5 | Fifteen Great Wildlife Viewing Trips

You don't have to travel halfway across the country for great wildlife viewing. Chances are, you'll find excellent viewing just a few miles from home. Nevertheless, there are several places in the United States that stand out as world-class wildlife viewing sites. Here's a list of some of my favorites.

Bighorn sheep, Georgetown Viewing Site, Georgetown, Colorado

Located along Interstate 70, approximately halfway between the cities of Denver and Vail, the Georgetown Viewing Site is among the most accessible places in the nation for viewing Rocky Mountain bighorn sheep. Between 175 and 200 bighorns occupy the rocky cliffs along the north side of Clear Creek Canyon. Fall and winter are the

best times to view or see them. Wildlife managers have constructed a tower shaped like a ram's horn from which people may view the sheep; the exhibit includes interpretive displays and mounted viewing scopes. Look closely; the sheep blend well with the terrain.

For more information, contact the Colorado Division of Wildlife, 6060 Broadway, Denver, CO 80216; phone (303) 297-1192. Be sure to purchase a copy of the division's *Bighorn Sheep Watching* guide for $3.

Alaskan brown bears, McNeil River State Game Sanctuary, Alaska

On the shores along Mifkik Creek and McNeil River Falls at the McNeil River State Game Sanctuary, Alaskan brown bears congregate to fish for migrating salmon. You'll see two to fifteen bears feeding here when the salmon run is on. Only ten people per day are allowed into the sanctuary to avoid disturbing the bears.

In June, viewing opportunities are at Mifkik Creek; the action moves to McNeil Falls in July and August with still more bears. Because of the extreme popularity of this viewing site, the Alaska Department of Fish and Game holds a lottery to select among hundreds of applicants.

Applications to the Alaska Department of Fish and Game must be postmarked no later than March 1 and arrive by March 15 of every year. Such a spectacular opportunity has its price: a $20 non-refundable application fee, and a user fee if you are selected ($100 for Alaska residents and $250 for nonresidents). Access to the site is by floatplane, which costs about $300 to charter. There are no facilities, so you must camp, and there is a four-mile-round-trip hike to the falls. Bringing children is not recommended.

To apply for this viewing chance of a lifetime, write the Alaska Department of Fish and Game, Wildlife Division, 333 Raspberry Road, Anchorage, AK 99518-1599; phone (907) 267-2179.

Manatees, Crystal River National Wildlife Refuge, Florida

The gentle, slow-moving endangered Florida manatee is a large aquatic mammal, typically ten feet long and weighing a thousand pounds. Manatees live in shallow, slow rivers, river mouths, estuaries, saltwater bays, and shallow coastal areas. In the United States, manatees have been found as far north as Virginia in summer; during winter, especially in cold weather, they congregate in warm-water discharges from power plants and warm springs, such as those found in Kings Bay, part of the Crystal River National Wildlife Refuge.

In recent years, more than two hundred manatees have used the Kings Bay area as wintering grounds. The bay offers unparalleled opportunities for viewing these gentle giants. Contact Crystal River National Wildlife Refuge, 1502 Southeast Kings Bay Drive, Crystal River, FL 34429; phone (904) 563-2088.

Rocky Mountain elk, Horseshoe Park, Rocky Mountain National Park, Colorado

During September and October, bull elk bugle as a physical release and to challenge other males during the fall rut. Listening to the bugle of an elk on a clear, crisp evening in the Rocky Mountains is an experience you will never forget. Bugling usually begins an hour before sunset and starts off as a low, hollow sound, rising to a high-pitched shriek, and culminating in a series of grunts.

One of the most reliable places to hear elk bugling in the fall is Horseshoe Park in Rocky Mountain National Park. Contact Rocky

Mountain National Park, Estes Park, CO 80517; phone (303) 586-1206.

Sandhill cranes, Platte River, Nebraska

For about five weeks in early spring (March), more than three-quarters of the world's population of sandhill cranes gathers along the Platte River in central Nebraska. You'll see more than 500,000 of these stately birds, resting and fattening up as they migrate back to breeding grounds in the Arctic.

The local chamber of commerce sponsors a three-day program/celebration (usually during the second weekend in March) known as "Wings over the Platte." Bus tours, viewing blinds, guided field trips, seminars, workshops, and wildlife art exhibits are featured. Contact Field Supervisor, U.S. Fish and Wildlife Service, 203 West Second Street, Grand Island, NE 68801; phone (308) 382-6468. Or contact Grand Island/Hall County Convention and Visitors Bureau at (800) 658-3178. Make hotel reservations well in advance.

California and Steller's sea lions, Sea Lion Caves, Oregon

Here, you will enter another world. After descending more than two hundred feet in an elevator to Sea Lion Caves on the coast of Oregon, you will find dim light, the hollow sound of waves crashing against cliffs, and the echoed barks of hundreds of Steller's sea lions (present year-round) and California sea lions (present from September to April). Sea lions swim and loaf below a cliff-top observation deck. Contact Sea Lion Caves, 91560 U.S. Highway 101, Florence, OR 97439; phone (503) 547-3111.

Gray whales, Channel Islands National Marine Sanctuary, California

The annual wintertime migration of the endangered gray whale brings these giant cetaceans directly off the coast of Southern California. Watching a gray whale thrust its fifty-foot-long body out of the water, rotate in midair, and crash back to the ocean will make your heart pound just a little bit faster. Some of the best whale-watching takes place aboard commercial boats that offer trips. But there are also good viewing opportunities from shore at the many points in the area: Point Conception, north of Santa Barbara; Point Dume in Malibu; and Point Loma in San Diego. In Ventura Harbor, visit the Channel Islands National Park Visitor Center: you'll find a viewing tower complete with spotting scopes for watching whales. Whales can be seen from December through April. Contact Channel Islands National Marine Sanctuary, 113 Harbor Way, Santa Barbara, CA 93109; phone (805) 966-7107.

For whale-watching boat trips contact the following:

- Bay Queen Harbor Cruises, 1691 Spinnaker Drive, Ventura Harbor, CA 93001; phone (805) 642-7753
- Island Packers, Inc., 1867 Spinnaker Drive, Ventura Harbor, CA 93001; phone (805) 642-1393
- Bailey's Tophat Charter, c/o Cisco's, Channel Islands Harbor, CA; phone (805) 985-8511
- Marina Sailing, 3600 South Harbor Boulevard, Channel Islands Harbor, CA; phone (805) 985-5219

Birds at Cape May, New Jersey

World-famous for its birding opportunities and ornithological research, Cape May, New Jersey, is considered one of the best birding sites in the world. From the southern tip of New Jersey, Cape May juts into Delaware Bay. Migrating birds are funneled here by geography; they stop to rest before making the eighteen-mile cross-bay flight.

More than four hundred species of birds have been recorded in the Cape May region. Large numbers of raptors (hawks, falcons, eagles) are regularly seen during fall migrations, as are songbirds (almost one hundred species). Visit the Cape May Bird Observatory, funded by the New Jersey Audubon Society, Box 3, Cape May Point, NJ 08212; phone (609) 884-2736.

J. N. "Ding" Darling National Wildlife Refuge, Florida

Boasting almost three hundred species of birds, more than fifty species of reptiles and amphibians, and more than thirty different species of mammals, "Ding" Darling National Wildlife Refuge is one of the most popular wildlife refuges in the nation. The refuge is located on Sanibel Island in southwest Florida. The site's five-mile, one-way auto tour offers excellent viewing. Plan to be at the observation tower at sunset in hopes of seeing roseate spoonbills flying overhead.

This refuge was named to commemorate Jay Norwood Darling, a pioneer in wildlife conservation. Darling's distinguished career included serving as head of the U.S. Biological Survey, forerunner of the U.S. Fish and Wildlife Service. He also initiated the Duck Stamp (Migratory Bird Hunting Stamp) and was a key figure in the establishment of the National Wildlife Refuge System. He won Pulitzer Prizes in 1923 and 1942 for his satirical conservation and political cartoons. Contact J.N. Ding Darling National Wildlife Refuge, 1 Wildlife Drive, Sanibel, FL 33957; phone (813) 472-1100.

Kirtland's warbler, Michigan

Six inches long, the endangered Kirtland's warbler is considered a large warbler. After wintering in the Bahamas, this bird returns each spring to a six-county area of Michigan's northern Lower Peninsula—the only place in the world where it nests. Fewer than six hundred breeding pairs of Kirtland's warblers exist, so viewing this rare, beautiful warbler is a thrill never to be forgotten.

The U.S. Fish and Wildlife Service and the Michigan Department of Natural Resources provide free daily tours of warbler habitat during May and June out of Grayling, Michigan. Contact U.S. Fish and Wildlife Service, Ecological Services Office, 1405 South Harrison Road, Room 302, East Lansing, MI 48823; phone (517) 337-6650. The USDA Forest Service provides daily tours out of Mio, Michigan; phone (517) 826-3252 for more information. If you want to head out on your own, drive the forty-eight-mile Jack Pine Wildlife Viewing Tour, beginning in Mio. Contact the Michigan Department of Natural Resources at (517) 826-3211.

Hawk Mountain Sanctuary, Pennsylvania

Migrating from breeding grounds in the northeastern United States and eastern Canada to wintering grounds in the southeastern United States, Mexico, and Central and South America, thousands of raptors pass over the rocky outcroppings of Hawk Mountain Sanctuary on Pennsylvania's Kittatinny Ridge during September and October.

Fourteen species routinely cross this ridge along the eastern flyway, including broad-winged hawks, sharp-shinned hawks, Cooper's hawks, bald eagles, and ospreys. Hawk Mountain regulars say the best viewing is usually between September 10 and September 25. Contact Hawk Mountain Sanctuary, Route 2, Kempton, PA 19529; phone (610) 756-6961.

Mexican free-tailed bats, Carlsbad Caverns National Park, New Mexico

On warm summer evenings in the Chihuahuan Desert, thousands of Mexican free-tailed bats exit in a whirling, smokelike column from the natural mouth of Carlsbad Caverns. An estimated 300,000 bats inhabit the caverns; they emerge at dusk to feed on moths and other night-flying insects, returning to the caverns before dawn. The best flights occur in late August and September, when young bats born in June join the evening ritual.

Bat Flight Amphitheater, located at the mouth of the cavern, seats up to a thousand people. Rangers give programs about the bats from Memorial Day to Labor Day prior to the evening flights. But don't expect to see bats if you visit in winter—they'll have migrated to Mexico. Contact Carlsbad Caverns National Park, 3225 National Parks Highway, Carlsbad, NM 88220; phone (505) 785-2232.

Bald eagles, Skagit River, Washington

One of the largest concentrations of wintering bald eagles in the lower forty-eight states occurs at the Skagit River Bald Eagle Natural Area in northern Washington State. More than three hundred bald eagles gather along the Skagit River to feed on spawned-out chum salmon, feeding along gravel bars between 7 A.M. and 11 A.M. Eagles feed here between November and early March, with peak numbers in mid-January. Contact The Nature Conservancy, Washington Field Office, 217 Pine Street, No. 1100, Seattle, WA 98101; phone (206) 343-4344. Or contact Mount Baker Ranger District, 2105 Highway 20, Sedro Woolley, WA 98284; phone (360) 856-5700. Also contact Washington Department of Wildlife, Region 4, Nongame Program, 16018 Mill Creek Boulevard, Mill Creek, WA 98012; phone (206) 775-1311.

Wintering elk, National Elk Refuge, Wyoming

Elk gather in one of the largest winter concentrations in the United States at the National Elk Refuge in Jackson, Wyoming. When snow comes to the high country in the region, elk migrate from high-elevation summer range to winter range in the valley. Almost 7,500 elk inhabit the area, staging America's version of an African plains scene, with thousands of animals stretched across the valley. Elk arrive in early November and return to the high country in early May.

In winter, visitors can view elk from a horse-drawn sleigh. Sleighs run from late December to March, 10 A.M. to 4 P.M. daily. Tours operate from the National Wildlife Art Museum, three miles north of Jackson on U.S. Highway 26/191. Contact the National Elk Refuge, 675 East Broadway, P.O. Box C, Jackson, WY 83001; phone (307) 733-9212.

Lesser prairie chickens, Comanche National Grassland, Colorado

With rapid, stomping feet, dropped wings, and raised neck feathers, the male prairie chicken conducts an elaborate dance to attract females for breeding. His ancient ritual can be observed from a blind or from your vehicle in a viewing area at the Comanche National Grassland, located near Campo, Colorado.

This courtship display can be seen from early March through mid-May. Arrive before daylight, be quiet, and never walk onto the birds' dancing grounds, known as leks. The best time to see the display is between sunrise and 9 A.M.—and you must remain in your vehicle, since prairie chickens are easily disturbed. If you plan on photographing from a blind, arrive one hour before daylight. Regulations say you must remain in the blind until at least one hour after sunrise. Contact the USDA Forest Service, P.O. Box 127, Springfield, CO 81073; phone (719) 523-6591. Call or write for a brochure and map. Be sure to make lodging reservations and check local road conditions before you visit.

IT'S A JUNGLE OUT THERE

*M*uch of my work involves research on public opinion on and attitudes toward natural resources. Agencies use this information to make better policy decisions; private companies use the information to develop marketing plans for their hunting, fishing, and wildlife viewing products. My staff conducts telephone and mail surveys, and personal interviews. Talking to people at times can be, er, . . . enlightening.

Once we were completing a telephone survey of attitudes toward animals when one of my interviewers read the standard introduction to a respondent. It went something like, "Hello, my name is Dianne and I'm calling from Responsive Management and we are conducting a short survey for the Illinois Department of Conservation on the use of animals . . ."

"On what?" came the reply from an elderly woman.

"The use of animals," said the interviewer.

"The WHAT?" said the woman again.

"The use of animals," replied the interviewer, now preparing for a very long interview.

"The use of ENEMAS?" came the response. "Why do you want to talk to me about the use of enemas?"

Another survey we conducted was on public attitudes toward the Florida panther, one of the most endangered mammals in the United States. Several interviewers told me that the following exchange occurred more than once:

"Hello, my name is Chris, and I'm calling from Responsive Management to ask about your opinions on the Florida panther."

Following a pause, the individual would reply, "Oh, I'd like to answer your survey but I'm not interested in hockey."

It didn't take us long to figure out that the professional hockey team in Florida is . . . you guessed it . . . the Florida Panthers.

In another survey, one of the issues was whether or not the public supported having an agency manage deer for trophy ➤

hunting. One gentleman never fully understood this question, and probably is still wondering why the state of Georgia is buying trophies for hunters.

Finally, not everyone answers our surveys. In another telephone survey we were conducting, a conversation went something like this:

"Hello, my name is David, and I'm calling on behalf of the department of natural resources, and we would like to ask you some questions on outdoor recreation."

"Sir, we don't go outside," the respondent answered, and hung up.

6 | Capturing
the Moment:
Wildlife photography

Many wildlife viewers are interested in photographing wildlife in the field. There are ways to get great photographic results without placing wildlife—or yourself—in jeopardy.

Vary Film Speeds

For best results with general wildlife photography, use medium-speed slide films such as ASA (ISO) 100 (Fujichrome or Ektachrome) or ASA 64 Kodachrome. For print film, use ASA 100 or 200. For landscape and scenic shots, use a slower-speed film such as Kodachrome 25, Velvia Fujichrome ASA 50, or Ektachrome 50 HC. Kodak's Ektar ASA 25 print film is excellent for enlargements.

Many photographers use film with an ASA of 100 or lower (known as "slow" film) because it enhances fine detail and won't appear grainy if enlarged. Slow film requires bright sunlight or a longer exposure time. For photographs in the early evening or early morning, use a faster film, rated ASA 250 or higher. Fast film is also better for moving animals, such as birds on the wing.

Early morning and late afternoon are the best times to photograph wildlife, for two reasons: wildlife is more apt to be active, and the quality of light at that time makes a better picture than the harsh light of midday.

Use the Right Lenses

Use a wide-angle lens (20 to 28 mm) to capture scenic shots. Use the greatest depth of field possible. Use a telephoto lens (200 to 400 mm) for the best close-up wildlife shots. Allowing space between the animals and the camera captures them more naturally and places them in their habitat.

A lens hood can help cut glare. It may also help protect the camera lens in the event it is bumped against another object.

Other Ideas

To produce sharp pictures, use a tripod. If shooting in dim light (early morning or late evening), consider using a shutter cable release. This will allow you to use a higher f-stop, which affords greater depth of field.

Take time to compose the shot.

Film and cameras should not be left in a closed vehicle during hot weather.

Stephen and Michele Vaughan, freelance writers and photographers from Colorado Springs, Colorado, contend, "The best equipment will not produce an outstanding image without an understanding of your subject. To become a good nature photographer, you must first become a good naturalist. The best way to learn about birds is to leave the camera bags behind, step into [the birds'] world and observe them. Educate yourself on where to find different species and how close to approach without spooking them."

The Reality Behind the Photograph

Laury Marshall, outdoor ethics director for the Izaak Walton League of America, points out the importance of understanding "the reality behind the photograph." Marshall remarks that many spectacular close-up shots of wildlife in books and magazines really weren't taken close-up, but were captured with a telephoto lens from a distance. Some of them show animals in a captive animal facility. She maintains that in many of the photographs appearing in magazines and books, the photographers appear to have been much closer than they actually were, giving a false impression to beginning wildlife photographers.

Chuck Bartlebaugh of the Center for Wildlife Information conveys how professional photographers get great photos:

■ They use captive and conditioned animals at game farms.

■ They photograph in controlled areas like Churchill (Canada) for polar bears, or the McNeil River Bear Sanctuary (Alaska) for grizzlies.

■ They use powerful telephoto lenses.

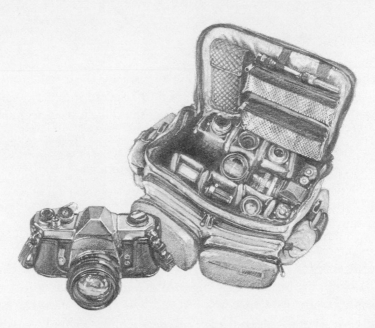

■ They are patient, devoting many years to getting desired photos in responsible ways.

Bartlebaugh notes, "Purchasing a camera does not give anyone permission to put animals, birds or marine life under stress."

"Another way professional photographers get great pictures is to shoot one heck of a lot of film," states Mark Hilliard, Watchable Wildlife Coordinator for the Bureau of Land Management. "If you only get one great picture out of a thousand, you've still got to shoot the thousand because you don't know whether the great photo will be the first shot, last shot, or one in between."

Safety Tips

Safety is a concern for wildlife photographers. As staff at Yellowstone National Park explained, "Photographers have been injured, and, on occasion, innocent bystanders [who were themselves maintaining a proper distance from the animals] were injured when the photographer caused the animal to charge."

Montana forester and photographer Bill Gabriel describes two gruesome episodes: "Two serious photographers with large telephoto lenses were killed by grizzly bears in Yellowstone and Glacier National Parks. . . . In the Glacier incident, film recovered from the camera of [the photographer] shows nearly forty photos of bears taken at various distances that indicated the bears had tried to move away, and he had followed them." In both episodes, the bear was a grizzly sow protecting her cubs.

Chuck Bartlebaugh offers the following guidelines for wildlife photographers who want to stay safe—and alive:

■ Photograph all animals from a vehicle or observation area, or at a distance with a 400 mm lens.

■ Remain alert to potential dangers despite your eagerness to take the perfect photo; maintain the recommended distance of five hundred to one thousand feet to avoid provoking large animals.

■ Never surprise an animal.

■ Retreat at any sign of stress or aggression.

■ Don't crouch or take a stance that may appear aggressive to a wild animal. Avoid following or chasing it; the animal may turn and charge.

■ Never surround an animal, crowd in on it, or try to herd it to a different location.

■ Never make unnecessary sounds to grab the animal's attention.

■ Stay out of dense brush. Avoid occupied dens and nests.

■ Be aware of other people in the area. Are their actions putting you in danger?

In nature photography there is one hard-and-fast rule of which the photographer must at all times observe the spirit: The welfare of the subject is more important than the photograph. This is not to say that photography should not be undertaken because of a slight risk to a common species. But the amount of risk which is acceptable decreases with the scarceness of the species, and the photographer should always do his utmost to minimize it.

"The Nature Photographer's Code of Practices"
by the Association of Natural History Photographic Societies

7 | Wildlife
for the
Future

Although every public opinion survey ever conducted on the subject shows that North Americans care deeply about wildlife and want to conserve and protect it, my research over the past decade has shown that very few people actually do anything to help wildlife. A citizenry that is concerned but does not act does not contribute to wildlife protection. Action counts.

People don't act on behalf of wildlife for several reasons. Sometimes people feel their efforts are futile. Some think that one

person can't make a difference. Others are too busy. One of the main reasons is that people don't really know what kinds of things they can do to help.

But believe this: Your efforts on behalf of wildlife are not futile. Little things can make a difference. Here are some big ways you can help assure wildlife's future:

Take a child birding, wildlife identifying, bug collecting, or wildlife photographing. Adult attitudes toward wildlife and the natural world are greatly influenced by childhood experiences. Nothing seems to foster positive attitudes toward wildlife more solidly than direct participation in wildlife-related activities at an early age.

Introduce a friend to wildlife viewing and birding. Research indicates there is an important link between birders (who actively identify species) and wildlife knowledge. In a national study on public attitudes toward wildlife, Dr. Stephen Kellert of Yale University concluded that the wildlife knowledge scores of committed birders were the highest of any demographic group examined in the entire study. The results suggested that active birding promotes an enhanced understanding of, awareness of, and concern for wildlife and the natural environment.

Buy yourself or a friend a copy of Aldo Leopold's *A Sand County Almanac*. Aldo Leopold is considered the father of wildlife management in America. His book *A Sand County Almanac*, written in the 1940s, is still the best book on wildlife ever written. By reading it, you will receive lessons on conservation, wildlife management, and ecology; the essays within it are written from the heart. Reading this book will give you a sense of our rich natural world.

Keep current on important wildlife issues facing your state or the nation. Check your local newspapers for information about current environmental issues. Read periodicals published by conservation groups. Here are a few worth checking out:

■ The National Wildlife Federation's *National Wildlife;* phone (703) 790-4000.

■ Defenders of Wildlife's *Defenders;* phone (202) 682-9400.

■ The National Audubon Society's *Audubon* or *Audubon Activist;* phone (212) 979-3000.

■ Izaak Walton League's *Outdoor Ethics Newsletter;* phone (301) 548-0150.

In addition, most state fish and wildlife agencies have magazines; nongame wildlife programs often publish newsletters. Check with your state fish and wildlife agency for availability.

Many other sources of information are available. Read as much as you can. Educate yourself, draw your own conclusions, and proceed accordingly. Only by getting into details can you support the right thing.

Write a letter. One of the most important actions a citizen can take also happens to be one of the easiest—writing letters. Letters to elected officials, such as your representative or senator, and letters to federal and state wildlife and environmental agencies can make a big difference. Your opinion counts. When officials receive enough letters about an issue, they do take notice.

Dan Witter of the Missouri Department of Conservation once told me about a conversation he'd had with a congressman. The congressman explained that he was surprised that a certain issue was such a hot topic and that so many people supported wildlife. Dan was surprised, too. "How many letters did you receive?" asked Dan. "Seven" was the reply.

Seven! Your opinion counts!

Most citizens think writing letters is a waste of time, and don't take advantage of this important wildlife conservation tool. The result? Public officials often don't know what people think about issues, and when they don't hear anything, they assume the public doesn't care.

Letters to elected officials in Washington helped pass important legislation for wildlife such as the Endangered Species Act, the Clean Water Act, and the Alaskan Lands Protection Act, which preserved millions of acres of land for wildlife. The National Wildlife Federation advises that the best time to write a letter to a legislator is before he or she must vote on a bill. The best time to write a letter to an environmental or wildlife agency is when a regulation has been proposed but not yet approved.

Be concise when you write. The National Wildlife Federation advises that you stick to one issue and use your own words—don't parrot something someone else has told you to say. Explain why you feel the way you do. It doesn't have to be technical, but explain how the issue affects you. Most importantly, ask the legislator or agency to do something specific: pass a regulation, vote for a particular bill, request hearings, or cosponsor a bill.

The letter needn't be typed, but write legibly. Ask for a reply.

You can contact a member of the U.S. House of Representatives by writing: The Honorable _____, U.S. House of Representatives, Washington, DC 20515. You can contact a U.S. Senator by writing: The Honorable_____, U.S. Senate, Washington, DC 20510. If you don't know the names of your senators or representatives, call your local library and ask them to find out for you. Give them the number of your voting district from your voter registration card, or tell them where you live, so they'll be able to identify your particular legislator.

Telephone your legislator. Telephone calls effectively relay last-minute messages to your state capitol or Washington, D.C. When you call, be polite and specific. Express your opinion, but also say what you want the legislator to do—vote for a particular issue, etc. Legislators keep tabs on their phone calls and tally calls and letters to gauge public opinion.

To reach your U.S. Senator or Representative by phone, call the Capitol switchboard at (202) 224-3121. The operator can furnish you with a needed number or connect you directly. To reach local legislators and officials, call your state government switchboard.

Write a letter to the editor of your newspaper. You'd be surprised how many opinion leaders, city officials, and citizens read the letters-to-the-editor section in newspapers. Elected officials often scan letters in local papers to assess public opinion. Before you write, get your facts straight and express your thoughts clearly. Be reasonable and avoid being preachy, and you will have a better chance of being published. Urge others to join you in doing something about the issue.

Meet with your legislator. Legislators meet with their constituents to stay in touch with their electors. Legislators need citizen support—that's how they get into office. Why not meet with your elected official about a wildlife issue and make your opinions known?

Report wildlife violators. If you know or even suspect that a wildlife law is being broken, report it to your state fish and wildlife agency. Most state agencies have toll-free numbers for reporting offenses, so the call won't cost anything. If you choose, you may remain anonymous and will not be required to appear in court. You may even get a reward if your report leads to an arrest. More importantly, you will have the satisfaction of knowing you have assisted wildlife law enforcement officers in catching poachers and others who abuse wildlife and wild habitats.

Donate to your state fish and wildlife agency's nongame wildlife program. Most state fish and wildlife agencies have a nongame wildlife program. Unlike a sportsman's program, this program manages wildlife areas for nonhunted species such as hawks, owls, frogs, and turtles. Many of these programs rely on donations to fund their conservation efforts. In many states, you can check off a box on your state income tax forms to donate to this cause as you file your state income tax.

Inquire about how your state funds its nongame wildlife program and share this knowledge with others. If you have an accountant prepare your taxes, tell him you would like to check the appropriate box and donate to the program.

Purchase a Migratory Bird Hunting Stamp (Duck Stamp) each year.
Proceeds from the sale of Duck Stamps purchase wetlands as wildlife refuges. Duck Stamp revenue goes directly to the acquisition of such land. Since 1934, the Duck Stamp program has conserved nearly four million acres of wetlands and other habitat. Duck stamps are sold at most post offices and most national wildlife refuges.

Landscape with native vegetation. Plant native vegetation around your home to attract wildlife, conserve water, and minimize fertilizer and pesticide use. Contact a local greenhouse or nursery to find sources for native plants. Your state fish and wildlife agency's nongame wildlife program or cooperative extension office can offer tips on getting started.

Volunteer for wildlife. Many state fish and wildlife agencies and private conservation groups rely on volunteers. You can volunteer to be an observer in the National Audubon Society's Christmas Bird Count. Each Christmas, more than 43,000 volunteers from all fifty states, every Canadian province, and territories and nations in the Caribbean, Central America, South America, and the Pacific count every bird and bird species seen during a twenty-four-hour period (from midnight to midnight). The entire count takes place during a two-and-a-half-week period beginning in mid-December. The Christmas Bird Count provides important trend data on bird populations. To participate, call the National Audubon Society at 700 Broadway, New York, NY 10003-9501; phone (212) 979-3083.

Save a snag. Many of America's cavity-nesting bird populations are declining. Eastern bluebirds, brown-headed nuthatches, red-headed woodpeckers, and northern flickers share one major reason for their decline: the loss of snags that provide foraging and cavities for nesting. Where safe and practical, let dead trees stand, and encourage your neighbors and others to do the same.

Build a nest box. Artificial nest boxes can enhance local cavity-nesting bird populations. There's an especially high demand for nest boxes to accommodate American kestrels and bluebirds. For instructions on how to build nest boxes, contact your state fish and wildlife agency. For information on how to build a bluebird nest box, contact the North American Bluebird Society, P.O. Box 6295, Silver Spring, MD 20906; phone (301) 384-2798.

Don't pick up "orphaned" animals. If you find an animal "left" alongside a road or in a field, it's probably not abandoned. The best thing you can do is leave it where it is. Its mother is more than likely watching from nearby, waiting for you to go.

Don't abandon a pet in the wild. Abandoned animals severely impact native wildlife, often killing wild animals in order to survive. Domestic cats can wreak havoc on backyard birds. Consider declawing your kitten/cat and keeping it inside. And don't dump those fish from your aquarium into natural waters; many species of fish can and have established themselves in North American lakes and streams, wreaking havoc on native fish populations.

Learn about pets before you buy them. Sometimes our love for animals can adversely affect wild populations. Some South American parrot populations have declined because of public demand for them as pets. When choosing a pet, pick captive-bred animals over wild ones. Learn if the pet of your dreams should stay where it naturally lives. Learn all you can about an animal and whether the pet trade affects its status in the wild. If it does, choose another species. For more information, contact TRAFFIC USA, World Wildlife Fund, 1250 24th Street NW, Washington, DC 20037; phone (202) 293-4800.

Don't buy animal products made from endangered species. Despite national and international laws regulating trade in endangered species, illegal imports still make their way to North America. Avoid purchasing ivory, buying products made from certain reptiles, and collecting corals; these activities may be bringing some forms of wildlife to the brink of extinction. For more information, contact TRAFFIC USA [see above].

Get a friend to join and support a conservation organization. The bright, energetic, and devoted staffs of North America's wildlife and conservation organizations count on you for support. If you don't belong to such an organization, join one. If you belong to one, join another. Get a friend to join, too. By doing so you not only support the organization financially, assisting its wildlife endeavors, but you also add important political clout. Politicians often judge organizations by the size of their membership. Imagine the president of the National Wildlife Federation being able to say, "I represent more than ten thousand members/supporters." Now imagine that president saying, "I represent four million Americans."

More than one thousand organizations actively work to protect North America's wildlife and environment. For a listing of these groups and their addresses, purchase the National Wildlife Federation's Conservation Directory by calling (800) 432-6564; ask for item #79561.

TAKING ACTION

*S*everal years ago, while working for a state fish and wildlife agency, I had the opportunity to evaluate my agency's wildlife education efforts. After a review, I saw clearly that the common theme we were sending citizens was that they should be concerned about wildlife. But after conducting several public opinion polls and a series of focus groups, I was forced to the conclusion that citizens were already concerned. What they weren't doing was acting on behalf of wildlife, and we weren't teaching them how.

My research indicated that citizens did not know specific things they could do. I concluded that the agency needed to publicize the ways people could help wildlife. I immediately went to work writing an article entitled, "Fifty Ways a Citizen Can Help Conserve Wildlife." After finishing the piece, I had to face a difficult fact: my article had to go through a lengthy agency review before it could be approved for publication. Since all of my previous articles and reports had been approved, I had an idea: I would submit the article for review while at the same time submitting the article to a magazine. I knew it would take several months for the article to hit the newsstands, and the agency review would take several months as well. I thought I would simply reduce by half the time it would take for my crucial message to reach the citizenry.

Imagine my excitement when the magazine editor called to say she loved the article and would publish it. Imagine my surprise when, the very next day, a rather perturbed division director stormed into my office and proceeded to reprimand me, saying it was inappropriate for a public employee to write an article on environmental action. The article would not be approved for publication.

110

➤ But . . . but . . . but . . .

I admitted that I had (somewhat hastily) submitted the article and that it would be published that month. The response was clear: publish the article and you might be looking for a new job. The editor wasn't happy when I asked that she pull the piece.

Bureaucracy did serve some purpose after all. After several discussions with the editor and the division director, we reached a compromise: the editor would publish the article without reference to my status as a public employee and get rid of a few of the more nocuous "ways a citizen can help wildlife." The article was eventually published with the title, "Twenty-Three Ways a Citizen Can Help Conserve Wildlife." The title didn't have the same ring as it had at the start. But I still had a job.

EPILOGUE

I wrote this book to help you get started watching wildlife. I intended to help you begin a lifelong pursuit of watching wild animals. I wanted to write a how-to guide but keep it simple and focused. In doing so, I was forced to exclude an enormous amount of detailed information, some of which you can find in field guides, magazines, books, and governmental literature. This book is only a beginning.

Throughout these pages, I've used larger, more glamorous species as examples of wildlife watching and its thrills. But we can observe all animals, and many times the best wildlife watching opportunities involve common species, many from our own backyards. If anything in this book compels you to notice something about wild animals, near or far, that you have never noticed before, I will have accomplished what I set out to do.

You will find that the more you learn about wildlife, the more you realize there is to learn. You will also find yourself perceiving more and more about our natural world; the seasons, different habitats, the numerous species that live around you. Many of these perceptions can never be adequately captured with words. Perhaps Aldo Leopold said it best when he wrote, "Our ability to perceive quality in nature begins, as in art, with the pretty. It expands through successive stages of the beautiful to values yet uncaptured by language. The quality of cranes lies, I think, in this higher gamut, as yet beyond the reach of words."

I write because I believe that North America's wildlife exists in delicate balance. We have destroyed wildlife and, in some cases, we have restored it. Bald eagles were in serious decline two decades ago because of human actions, but they now appear to be on their way to recovery because of human efforts. Having inherited a rich and glorious world from our ancestors, we now have the critical responsibility to safeguard it for our children and grandchildren. Theodore Roosevelt, one of America's eminent conservationists, phrased it best when he said, "Wild beasts and birds are by right not the property merely of the people alive today, but the property of unborn generations, whose belongings we have no right to squander."

LIST OF ILLUSTRATIONS

ABOUT THE AUTHOR

Wildlife biologist Mark Damian Duda has traveled extensively, from the Everglades in south Florida to Denali National Park in Alaska, to watch and photograph wildlife. His first-hand experiences watching orcas off the coast of British Columbia, grizzly bears in Alaska, bighorn sheep in Colorado, black bears in Tennessee, snow geese in Virginia, and humpback whales off the coast of California have instilled in him a strong desire to teach others how to view wildlife successfully and ethically.

Mark is the executive director of Responsive Management, an international natural resource consulting firm that assists natural resource, environmental, and outdoor recreation organizations, helping them to better understand their customers and constituents. He has worked as a consultant to more than forty state fish and wildlife agencies, and for the U.S. Fish and Wildlife Service, the Canadian Wildlife Service, USDA Forest Service, Bureau of Land Management, International Association of Fish and Wildlife Agencies, and many private conservation groups, including the Izaak Walton League of America, Wildlife Management Institute, and the American Sportfishing Association.

Mark is a noted authority on wildlife viewing, and a regular speaker at Watchable Wildlife Program conferences. He has been instrumental in initiating and developing wildlife viewing programs and enthusiasm nationwide. Author of more than fifty papers, book chapters, journal articles, and scientific reports on wildlife viewing and conservation, he is also the author of the *Virginia Wildlife Viewing Guide*.

Mark was named Conservation Educator of the Year by the Florida Wildlife Federation and the National Wildlife Federation and was the recipient of the Western Association of Fish and Wildlife Agencies 1995 Special Conservation Achievement Award. He holds a master's degree from Yale University in natural resource policy and planning and is a native Virginian living in the Shenandoah Valley. He can be reached at Responsive Management, P.O. Box 389, Harrisonburg, VA 22801.

FALCON GUIDES

THE WATCHABLE WILDLIFE SERIES
Arizona Wildlife Viewing Guide
California Wildlife Viewing Guide
Colorado Wildlife Viewing Guide
Florida Wildlife Viewing Guide
Idaho Wildlife Viewing Guide
Indiana Wildlife Viewing Guide
Iowa Wildlife Viewing Guide
Kentucky Wildlife Viewing Guide
Montana Wildlife Viewing Guide
Nevada Wildlife Viewing Guide
New Mexico Wildlife Viewing Guide
North Carolina Wildlife Viewing Guide
North Dakota Wildlife Viewing Guide
Oregon Wildlife Viewing Guide
Tennessee Wildlife Viewing Guide
Texas Wildlife Viewing Guide
Utah Wildlife Viewing Guide
Vermont Wildlife Viewing Guide
Virginia Wildlife Viewing Guide
Washington Wildlife Viewing Guide
Wisconsin Wildlife Viewing Guide

BIRDER'S GUIDES
Birding Arizona
Birder's Guide to Montana
Birding Minnesota

SCENIC DRIVING GUIDES
Scenic Byways
Scenic Byways II
Back Country Byways
Arizona Scenic Drives
California Scenic Drives
Colorado Scenic Drives
Montana Scenic Drives
New Mexico Scenic Drives
Oregon Scenic Drives
Scenic Driving Georgia
Texas Scenic Drives
Traveler's Guide to the Lewis & Clark Trail
Traveler's Guide to the Oregon Trail
Traveler's Guide to the Pony Express Trail

ROCKHOUND'S GUIDES
Rockhounding Arizona
Rockhound's Guide to California
Rockhound's Guide to Colorado
Rockhound's Guide to Montana
Rockhound's Guide to New Mexico
Rockhound's Guide to Texas

■ *To order any of these books, or to request an expanded list of available titles, including guides for viewing wildlife, birding, scenic driving, or rockhounding, please call 1-800-582-2665, or write to Falcon, PO Box 1718, Helena, MT 59624.*

take time to learn more

With this **VIDEO**, a companion to the book, *Watching Wildlife*, you'll discover the best and latest techniques for viewing wildlife in natural surroundings. Take time to learn more and increase your chances of seeing wild animals on any outdoor excursion.

what you'll discover:

- Techniques for seeing animals without disturbing them.
- Where and when to go for the best viewing.
- Ideas for including children on wildlife viewing trips.
- How to identify tracks and other signs of wildlife activity.

Watching Wildlife Video
A Guide to One of America's Most Popular Activities
VHS, 30 minutes. $19.95

To order or to request a catalog,
please call 1-800-582-2665